WOMEN IN CLASS. ....

Current and forthcoming titles in the Classical World Series

Classical World Series

WOMEN IN CLASSICAL ATHENS

Sue Blundell

Bristol Classical Press

General Editor: John H. Betts
Series Editor: Michael Gunningham

For my mother, Nora Blundell,
with much love

Cover illustration: Woman making offering of ointment or jewellery
from a mid-fifth century *stele*, Staatlichemuseum, Berlin.

First published in 1998 by
Bristol Classical Press
an imprint of
Gerald Duckworth & Co. Ltd
61 Frith Street
London W1D 3JL
e-mail: inquiries@duckworth-publishers.co.uk
Website: www.ducknet.co.uk

Reprinted 2001 (twice)

A catalogue record for this book is available
from the British Library

ISBN 1-85399-543-6

Printed in Great Britain by
Antony Rowe Ltd, Eastbourne

Contents

Acknowledgements

A number of passages in this book have been 'tested' on students studying for the MA in Classical Civilisation at Birkbeck College, University of London. Thanks are owed to them for their comments and suggestions, and in general for the spirited support which they have extended to the downtrodden women of Athens over the past fifteen months. Visual images of women form an important element in the book, and I am indebted to the British Academy for helping to extend my knowledge of this topic; the Small Personal Research Grant which it awarded me in 1992 enabled me to study important collections of Greek vases in Germany and the USA. Among the many colleagues and friends whose ideas about gender and representation have been a stimulus and an inspiration, I would like to mention in particular Michael Duigan, Margaret Williamson and Andrew Wyllie. I am grateful to all of them for many hours of delightful conversation. I must also thank Brian Sparkes and Carolyn Jones for much needed help with illustrations, and Michael Gunningham, of the Bristol Classical Press, for the patience, care and enthusiasm with which he has fulfilled the role of editor. Special thanks go, as ever, to Nick Bailey.

List of Illustrations

Chapter 1
Introduction

The goddess and her temple

In 447 BC work began on a new temple on the Acropolis, the sacred hill which dominated the centre of Athens. The temple was being built to replace the shrines which Persian invaders had destroyed when they sacked the city in 480 BC. It was to be dedicated to Athena, patron and protector of the people of Athens, and would house a colossal statue of the goddess covered in leaves of ivory and gold. Over twelve metres in height, the statue when completed showed the patron deity as a warrior figure equipped with massive helmet and shield. Later it acquired the name of *Parthenos*, or Maiden, in acknowledgement of Athena's status as a virgin goddess. The temple itself was the largest ever constructed on the Greek mainland, and soon became known as the Parthenon.

In Athens, then, a female warrior towered above a city in which women played no part in either warfare or politics. On the Athenian Acropolis a magnificent temple was erected to a divine virgin by a society which regarded marriage and childbirth as the only significant roles available to a respectable woman. Athena was a highly conspicuous goddess whose name was often on men's lips, yet in the community in which she was worshipped a leading statesman could announce to a large public gathering:

'The greatest glory of a woman is to be least talked about among men, whether in praise or blame.'
(Pericles' funeral speech, THUCYDIDES 2.46)

Clearly the Athenian notion of femininity involved some striking contradictions. One of the purposes of this book is to examine these contradictory attitudes, and to consider from a number of angles the question of what women meant to men in Classical Athens. Its other purpose is to explore what it meant to be a woman – to gain an understanding of women's everyday lives, their relationships with family and friends, and the place which they occupied in Athenian society.

The discussion takes as its starting point the sculptures which decorated the Parthenon. Though these are dominated by images of men, all the scenes have females in them too, and these figures will provide a framework for the wider investigation of real and invented women. The survey will make use of material from a wide variety of sources, including statues, paintings on pots, plays, law-court speeches, historical writings, and philosophical and medical treatises. Unfortunately, all these works were produced by male artists and authors. The only women writers from ancient Greece who are known to us are poets (Sappho is the most famous), and none of these seems to have lived in Classical Athens. So Athenian women are unable to speak for themselves, and as a result much of what we learn about their lives is coloured by male misunderstandings or prejudices.

There are also enormous gaps in our knowledge. Some areas of women's experience were either kept hidden from men or did not interest them, so they were never discussed. We also have to bear in mind that most of our information relates to relatively well-off females, and that the lives of slaves, immigrants, and poor citizen women, about which we know much less, would in many ways have been very different. Yet in spite of all these limitations there are many features of women's existence which we can attempt to reconstruct; and though male attitudes are often unavoidable these are often worth studying in their own right, for they have much to tell us about an influential male-dominated culture.

When the Parthenon was being built Athens was one of the most prosperous and powerful states in the Greek world, and the new temple was designed to reflect this prestige. Constructed entirely from marble and rich in sculptural decoration, it served as a memorial to Athens' past achievements in repelling the Persians, and as a highly visible emblem of her current status as a political and cultural leader among the Greeks. Through the Parthenon the Athenians were advertising their greatness both to themselves and to the city's many visitors; but at the same time they were honouring the gods who had helped them attain this greatness. Above all they were paying homage to Athena, their divine protector and the symbol of their strength.

Athens' position in the Greek world was by no means unchallenged, and it would be quite wrong to think of the city as the Greek capital, for in the classical period Greece was never a united country. There is no doubt, however, that during the fifth century BC the Athenians were living in an affluent and enterprising community which was able to foster a remarkable degree of creativity among its thinkers, writers and artists. Even in the fourth century, when the power of Athens was beginning to fade, the cultural output of the city was still outstanding. In the section which follows we shall be examining the political and economic background to this achievement (see also Fig. 1).

EVENTS AND PEOPLE: A TIME CHART

BC	
490	First Persian invasion of Greece. Battle of Marathon.
480	Second Persian invasion. Sack of Athens. Battle of Salamis.
479	Battle of Plataea, and retreat of the Persians.
478-7	Athens founds the Delian League. In the following years this develops into the Athenian empire.
472	Aeschylus' tragedy *The Persians* performed.
468	Sophocles' first prize-winning tragedy performed.
450s	Pericles becomes a leading politician, and introduces reforms which add the finishing touches to the democratic system.
458	Aeschylus' trilogy the *Oresteia* performed.
455	Euripides' first tragedy performed.
451	Pericles introduces a law to restrict citizenship.
447-32	Parthenon constructed.
440-20	Historian Herodotus active.
431	Euripides' tragedy *Medea* performed. Outbreak of the Peloponnesian War. Rural population brought into the city. Thucydides begins his history of the War.
429	Death of Pericles.
427	Aristophanes' first comedy staged.
421-13	Temporary peace with Sparta.
415-13	An Athenian expedition against Sicily, ending in catastrophic defeat.
413	Peloponnesian War breaks out again.
411	Aristophanes' comedy *Lysistrata* performed.
404	Athenians defeated by the Spartans, and lose their empire, navy, and democracy.
403	Democracy restored.
400	Lysias composes a speech for Euphiletos.
399	Philosopher Socrates executed.
386	Plato founds his philosophical school the Academy. His dialogue *The Republic* published soon afterwards.
371	Spartans defeated by the Thebans at Leuktra.
370-30	Praxiteles active as a sculptor.
362	Xenophon's *Household management* published.
354	Demosthenes' first public speech.
338	Philip II of Macedon wins the battle of Chaironea, and takes over the whole of mainland Greece.
336	Philip assassinated, and succeeded by Alexander.

Fig. 1 Time chart for Classical Athens (some dates are approximate).

Athens in the classical period

The word 'classical' is conventionally used to denote the period in Greek history which begins in 500 BC and ends in 336, the date when Alexander the Great became the ruler of Macedonia. It refers therefore to the whole of the fifth century (500-400 BC) and a large part of the fourth. This was a time when Greeks in general were experiencing some far-reaching political, social and cultural changes.

The Greek world included not only mainland Greece and the islands, but also a large number of settlements established by Greeks in western Turkey, southern Italy, and Sicily, and more scattered communities in Spain, France, north Africa and along the shores of the Black Sea. By 500 BC Greeks in all these regions were living in political units known as *poleis* (singular, *polis*). In physical terms a *polis* was an area of agricultural land with an urban centre, where many of the inhabitants lived and where they also met to trade their goods, make collective decisions, and worship their gods. Most *poleis* were quite small, with populations in the low thousands, but all of them were independent, self-governing states. Athens was one of the largest, both in territorial and in population terms. It consisted of a rural area known as Attica, which was about the size of the county of Somerset, and a city centre; and by about 430 BC its total population may have numbered between 250,000 and 300,000. This figure included not only citizens and their families, but also slaves and resident aliens. Each citizen lived in a unit known as an *oikos*, which can be translated as family, house, home, or household – the word describes a building and the land attached to it, and the family members and slaves who lived there. Although Athens became an important trading state in the fifth century, and also had some profitable manufacturing industries, most of the population still earned their living from farming.

By the beginning of the fifth century BC mainland Greece was beginning to attract the attention of the Persians, who at this time controlled an enormous empire extending from Egypt in the west to Pakistan in the east. In 490 the Persian king Darius launched a relatively small-scale invasion of Greek territory, which was halted by the victory of the Athenian forces at the battle of Marathon. Ten years later his son Xerxes led a massive army into Greece and occupied over half the mainland, including Athens. Spartan and Athenian forces played a vital part in the two decisive victories, at Salamis in 480 and Plataea in 479, which finally turned back this invasion. Their remarkable success in overcoming the threat from the Persians was to give the Greeks tremendous confidence in their own political institutions and values.

In the following years Athens took advantage of the collapse of Persian power in the Aegean area in order to create a naval alliance called the Delian league. Its members included most of the Greek states on the islands and along the west coast of Turkey. The league was dominated by Athens right from the start, and it soon began to be referred to as the Athenian empire. Its navy was increasingly employed to further Athenian trading interests, and by Greek standards Athens became very prosperous. The wealth acquired in this way made a vital contribution to the city's cultural achievements, and it also helped to underpin the operations of its democratic system. This attained its most radical form around the middle of the fifth century. Its hallmark was its participative character. All major decisions were made by an Assembly which all adult male citizens were entitled to attend, and most administrative and judicial functions were performed by men who were chosen annually by lot from the entire citizen body. It was a remarkable system, but it only ever embraced a minority of the population, the citizen elite. Resident aliens, slaves and women were all excluded.

The naval power which Athens wielded in the Aegean area was matched on the mainland by the domination exercised by the *polis* of Sparta through its disciplined and professional army. The two states frequently clashed, and in 431 a major conflict, the Peloponnesian War, broke out. The confrontation had a tremendous effect on lifestyles and patterns of thought in Athens. In spite of some initial successes it ended in total defeat for the Athenians. In 404 they were forced to surrender their empire and most of their navy; but after a bitter internal struggle they managed to retain their democratic system.

The war had destroyed the balance of power in the Greek world, and in the century which followed a number of states vied for leadership. These wrangles were brought to an end by Philip II, the ruler of Macedonia in northern Greece. By the middle of the fourth century he had equipped himself with a highly efficient army, which he employed in a series of incursions into the rest of Greece. In 338 his victory over Athenian and Theban forces at the battle of Chaironea put him in control of the whole of the mainland, and the political independence of the Greek *poleis* was now at an end. Two years later Philip was assassinated, and his son Alexander succeeded him. His activities were soon to transform the Greek world, and the classical period was now at an end.

Female figures in the Parthenon sculptures

Like other classical temples, the Parthenon consisted of a rectangular chamber, called a cella, which contained the statue of the deity. At either end there was a porch supported on columns. More columns were added in an outer colonnade which went all the way round the cella and porches, and the entire building was covered by a pitched roof (Figs. 2 and 3). Sculpture was applied to three principal elements, described in the chart in Fig. 4 (p. 8). Although a great deal of damage has been done over the years, large sections of these sculptures survive, and most of them can be viewed today in the British Museum.

The figures depicted in the sculptures belong to three different levels of being. Those in the **pediments** are mostly deities. The majority of the **metopes** show mythological characters who are human rather than divine – men and women who performed marvellous deeds in the distant past. In the **frieze** the sculptors were representing human beings of their own day and age, though they must be seen as ideal types rather than real-life individuals. Three sides of the frieze are occupied by the Athenian men who took part in the Panathenaic procession. But in the east section, where the Olympian deities sit waiting to receive their worshippers, the two strands of the procession are headed by women (Fig. 5, p. 9).

Most of this book will be devoted to this last group of females, the Athenian women of the citizen class who lived in the fifth and fourth centuries BC. In Chapter 2 we shall be looking at the unmarried girls who are present at the gathering, while Chapter 3 will examine their married companions. The last three chapters are much shorter. Chapter 4 deals with the females from the Parthenon's other two levels of being, the goddesses and the characters from myth. In Chapter 5 we shall turn our attention to the women who are given no place at all in the sculptures – the foreigners and slaves who played a vital part in the life of the city, but were generally forgotten when public monuments were being erected. Finally, Chapter 6 presents some overall conclusions about the Athenian notion of femininity, and the impact which this had on the real-life women of Classical Athens.

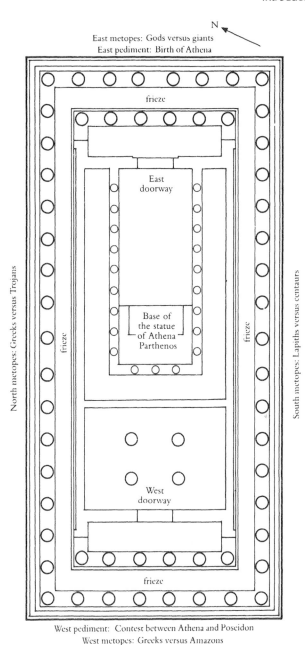

N

East metopes: Gods versus giants
East pediment: Birth of Athena

frieze

East
doorway

Base of
the statue
of Athena
Parthenos

West
doorway

frieze

North metopes: Greeks versus Trojans

frieze

South metopes: Lapiths versus centaurs

frieze

West pediment: Contest between Athena and Poseidon
West metopes: Greeks versus Amazons

Fig. 2 Plan of the Parthenon, showing the position of the sculptures.

Fig. 3 View of the Parthenon from the west end. The contest between Athena and Poseidon was depicted in the pediment, and the metopes below showed the battle between Greeks and Amazons.

THE PARTHENON SCULPTURES

The pediments   The triangular gables at either end of the building.

West end: Athena's victory over the god Poseidon in a contest held to decide which of them should be patron deity of Athens.

East end: Athena's birth from the head of her father Zeus, and her reception by a group of deities.

The metopes   Separate rectangular sculptures above the outer colonnade on all four sides of the building.

West end (below the pediment): the battle between the Greeks and the Amazons.

North side: the sack of Troy by the Greeks.

South side: the battle between the Lapiths and Centaurs (Fig. 22).

East end (below the pediment): the battle between the Gods and the Giants.

The frieze   A continuous band of sculpture which extended above the porches and along the external walls of the *cella*.

The subject: a religious procession, almost certainly the one staged every four years at the Great Panathenaia, a festival of Athena.

The east section of the frieze: the two strands of the procession converge on a group of twelve Olympian deities.

Fig. 4 Parthenon sculptures chart.

Fig. 5 Women walking in the Panathenaic procession, from the east section of the Parthenon frieze: slab VIII, c.440 BC.

Chapter 2
Unmarried women

Growing up in Athens

Just over half of the women in the Parthenon frieze appear to be unmarried. They are distinguished from their companions by their long hair and their style of dress, but not by their figures, which seem to be fully developed. This suggests that they were to be seen as either approaching puberty or having just passed it, which in either case would have meant that in the fairly near future they were going to be married. So they were at an age when ordinarily they would have been quite carefully supervised and protected from male attention. In spite of this, at the Great Panathenaia they were positioned right at the head of an important religious procession, and would have had thousands of eyes fixed upon them.

The young women who were awarded this honour would probably have felt very nervous, for in their day-to-day lives they would have had little experience of performing in public. From about the age of six many Athenian boys attended small private schools and also visited the civic gymnasia. Girls stayed at home with their mothers, and would have had far fewer opportunities for socialising with members of their own sex. In affluent upper class families daughters may have been kept indoors most of the time, especially as they got older. In one of Euripides' tragedies Antigone is allowed to go up to the roof of her parents' house to get a view of the army assembled below, but a slave has to do a preliminary reconnoitre:

> in case one of the townspeople appears in the roadway,
> and you are involved in a scandal...
> (EURIPIDES, *The Phoenician Women* 93-4)

In spite of their lack of formal education some girls must have learned from their mothers how to read, for there are vase-paintings which show women holding book-scrolls. In wealthier families girls may even have had lessons in singing and lyre-playing; but literate women would certainly have been in the minority. There may have been quite a few Athenian men who thought, along with a character in one comic play, that teaching a woman to read and write was tantamount to giving additional poison to a horrible snake ([MENANDER] fragment 702, Kock).

Most girls' education would have taken the form of working alongside their mothers and learning skills such as cooking and wool-working; and it would not have been long before they were practising these skills in earnest. At the stage in life when young Athenian men were still receiving instruction in their civic and military duties, the majority of young women were already married.

As the Parthenon frieze indicates, however, girls did not lead totally sheltered lives before their marriages. Even young women who were so bashful that they were 'ashamed to be seen even by relatives' (LYSIAS 3.6-7) would have been expected to shed their modesty and appear in public when performing important religious tasks. In most of these the girls were honouring the various goddesses worshipped in Athens. For example, a number of girls called *arktoi* or 'bears' lived in a sanctuary of Artemis at Brauron on the east coast of Attica, possibly for as long as a year. While they were there they ran races and took part in 'bear-dances' in honour of the goddess. According to legend, this service was an atonement for the slaughter by some Athenian youths of a bear sacred to Artemis, a deity whose close relationship with the natural world involved her in the care of young animals. Other important duties were undertaken by the *arrhephoroi*, or 'bearers of secret things', girls who lived for a time on the Acropolis, and performed secret rites for Aphrodite in a sanctuary at the foot of the hill. Another of their tasks was to help set up the loom for the weaving of the *peplos* or robe presented to the goddess Athena at the climax of the Panathenaic procession (Fig. 6, p. 12). The girls carrying stools who appear in the centre of the eastern section of the Parthenon frieze are often identified as *arrhephoroi*. Athena's robe was actually woven by more young women known as *ergastinai*, or 'workers', and some of these may be shown among the female figures walking at the front of the procession. *Kanephoroi* ('basket-bearers') were girls who in religious processions carried baskets containing sacred objects. We know that in real life some of them participated in the Great Panathenaia, but they do not seem to be shown in the frieze.

These are just a few of the important religious tasks undertaken by young Athenian women before they were married. Most of them were connected in some way with their future roles as wives and mothers, and were carried out for goddesses who would help them perform these roles. Aphrodite, for example, was the deity responsible for a woman's sexuality, while Artemis was among other things a goddess of childbirth, and one of Athena's functions was the supervision of the quintessentially feminine activities of spinning and weaving. However, the significance of these religious rituals was not confined to the individuals who performed them. By honouring the goddesses who protected their *polis* the young women were also helping to secure the well-being and prosperity of the community as a whole.

Fig. 6 Part of the east section of the Parthenon frieze: slab V, c.440 BC. Left to right: female attendant (possibly one of the *arrhephoroi*), carrying a stool on her head; priestess (probably of Athena); male official and a child (a temple servant?), holding the *peplos*; Athena; Hephaistos.

Axiothea in the Academy

In Athens religion was the only area of public activity in which women played a prominent part. Yet not all Athenian men thought that women should be excluded from education, or from the political duties which citizens undertook when their education was complete. The philosopher Plato in his dialogue the *Republic*, written in the 380s BC, presents a model of an ideal state in which only those people who have achieved philosophical knowledge of the Good are to qualify as rulers. Plato believes that the only innate differences between males and females are those which relate to sexual reproduction, and that these should not prevent women from participating on an equal footing with men in the government of the state. Consequently, the education which is provided for potential rulers should be open to females. They will receive physical as well as intellectual instruction, and will exercise naked in the gymnasium alongside the men. Like their male companions these women can aspire to the highest offices of state, and their work will not be interrupted to any great extent by the burdens of child-care. Once they have given birth their babies will be placed in state-run nurseries, where they will be brought up by nurses drawn from outside the ruling class.

> State officials will arrange for children to be breast-fed by bringing their mothers into the nurseries, making absolutely sure that no mother recognises her own child;...and all the sitting up at night and all the hard work will be handed over to the nurses.
>
> (PLATO, *Republic* 460 c-d)

This revolutionary and highly imaginative programme relied heavily on the notion that child-care could not be easily combined with service to the community. If women were to play a part in public life, Plato believed, they would have to surrender the mothering role completely. But only an elite group of females would ever be placed in this position. The great majority of women would continue to carry out their traditional nurturing functions, and it would be from this sector of society that the state would draw its supply of nurses. In Plato's ideal state only top women would ever be eligible for the top jobs.

It is doubtful whether many Athenian women would have found Plato's scheme of things particularly appealing and in Athens, needless to say, there was never any likelihood that it would ever be put into practice; but it seems that some females from other parts of Greece were attracted by the philosopher's more egalitarian approach. Later writers tell us that Plato's philosophical school, the Academy, included two women among its pupils, and that one of them, Axiothea, left her home in Arcadia and came to live in Athens after reading the *Republic*. She attended lectures at the Academy dressed as a man, and by this ploy she was able to escape notice (DIOGENES LAERTIUS 3.46; THEMISTIUS, *Orations* 295e). It is possible that Axiothea really did have to resort to disguise in order to get into the Academy. But whether true or not, her brief biography served to reinforce the popular belief that women who wanted to take part in 'men's' activities were bound to sacrifice their femininity and assume a masculine identity. Much the same might be said of Plato's female rulers in the *Republic*. When they were awarded an equal place in government they were at the same time transformed by the philosopher into honorary men, with only a minimal involvement in the usual activities of Greek women.

Body images and body coverings

The story of Axiothea is one of many in which the theme of cross-dressing is used to highlight a person's assumption of a role normally undertaken by the opposite sex. Transvestism on the part of both males and females is often used in myth and fiction as a way of drawing attention to activities which in some way disturb the conventional division of labour between the sexes. Women's adoption of men's dress generally signals their incursion into the masculine fields of warfare or politics. For example, the gender-bending behaviour of the warrior goddess Athena is advertised by the fact that she rarely appears in public without her helmet, shield or spear (Fig. 7). In Aristophanes' comedy *Women in the Assembly* female conspirators who are plotting to take over the government of Athens infiltrate a meeting of the democratic assembly disguised as men, wearing cloaks, shoes and walking-sticks filched from their husbands. In real life transvestism was an occasional feature of religious ceremonies, most notably those associated with rites of passage. Young men who dressed up as girls at their coming-of-age may have been displaying the sexually ambivalent qualities which they were soon to renounce when they entered manhood and became full citizens of Athens.

However, there was certainly no general trend towards cross-dressing in Classical Athens – there was no Athenian equivalent of the fashion for trousers which in 1960s Britain was a visible sign of women's changing lifestyle. There may have been a few females however who, like Axiothea, were forced to conceal themselves in masculine clothing in order to survive in a man's world. In another story we hear about a woman named Hagnodike who had her hair cropped and wore a man's tunic so that she could study medicine. Still disguised as a man, she established a very successful practice in obstetrics, but was eventually brought to court on a charge of sexual corruption. Her rivals were jealous of her success with her female patients and decided that she must be seducing them.

> At the point when she was about to be sentenced by the court, Hagnodike lifted up her tunic and demonstrated to the jurors that she was a woman. Her prosecutors then became even more vigorous in their accusations. But some of the wives of the jurors came to the court, and announced, 'You are no longer our husbands but our enemies, if you are prepared to condemn a woman who has done so much for our health'. After this the Athenians changed the law, so that women of Athenian birth were allowed to study medicine.   (HYGINUS, *Fabulae* 274)

The Parthenon sculptures contain one striking example of the theme of cross-dressing, in the scenes at the West end where the Amazons are represented. These mythological female warriors will be discussed in Chapter 4. The real-life women who appear in the Parthenon frieze are wearing

Fig. 7 Athena emerging from the head of her father Zeus. A black-figure amphora, or storage-jar, of the mid-sixth century BC.

conventional feminine garb, of course; but here too clothing is an important consideration. Differences in dress and hairstyles act as markers of the women's identity, because they serve to distinguish the unmarried girls from their older married companions. The Greek tendency to idealise the human body meant that physical signs of ageing, such as creases and wrinkles, were rarely shown by artists. But sometimes age differences between women were important enough to be indicated through other devices. In the Parthenon frieze, where hairstyle and clothing are still recognisable, we see women with long hair wearing garments called *peploi* and shoulder-mantles (the last three women in Fig. 5, p. 9), while the women with their hair up are dressed in the tunic known as the *chiton* and longer cloaks called *himatia* (the first woman in Fig. 5). The former, it is believed, are the women who are not yet married. Perhaps the designers of the sculptures wanted to highlight the way in which various women – both unmarried and married, young and old – were being brought together within the procession, united by their devotion to Athena.

Only unmarried women regularly wore their hair loose or in a long plait. This custom may well have contributed to the widespread notion that girls were naturally wild and exuberant. In ancient Greece it was commonly believed that females in general were prone to excessive and uncontrolled behaviour, and that they were therefore badly in need of male guidance, provided first by their fathers and later by their husbands. When women temporarily broke free from these restraints they were represented by male artists as literally letting their hair down. For example, women worshippers who left the city to perform ecstatic dances for the god Dionysos in the mountains were shown in vase-paintings with long flowing locks (Fig. 8). In his tragedy the *Bacchae* Euripides describes these devotees as 'letting their hair stream down over their shoulders' (EURIPIDES, *Bacchae* 695). In unmarried girls the wildness which went with their long hair was probably seen as permissible, but it also demonstrated the need to provide them with husbands before their fathers grew too old to control them.

This idea of the unruly nature of the female is also conjured up by the use of imagery which associates women with animals. Young women of marriageable age were often called 'fillies' (eg. EURIPIDES, *Andromache* 621), and it was thought that they needed to be 'tamed' or 'yoked' in marriage (EURIPIDES, *Medea* 804; HOMER, *Iliad* 18.432). A similar metaphor is present in the name *arktoi* given to the girls who served Artemis at Brauron. The freedom which the girls were given to 'act the bear' during their stay with the goddess may have been seen as a way of getting their wildness out of their systems, a vital preliminary to marriage. Artemis herself, a hunting deity who loved to roam untamed stretches of mountain and forest, was a young unmarried virgin with more than a touch of savagery about her. An acknowledgment of this aspect of femininity, expressed through the physical exhilaration of the girls' service to the goddess, may have been the price which Artemis demanded before she would allow young women to surrender themselves in matrimony.

When women married they began to put their hair up in a chignon or coil, one sign that they had given up their earlier undisciplined existence.

Another sign was a change in their style of dress, although there were certainly no firm rules about this. In the frieze most of the unmarried women are heavily draped in short mantles, an overgarment – the *peplos* – and a sleeved undergarment. The *peplos* (see Fig. 9, p. 18) consisted of a single rectangle of woollen material which was wrapped around the

Fig. 8 A maenad. In her right hand she carries a *thyrsos*, a sacred wand of Dionysos, and in her left she is wielding a small panther. The interior of a white-ground cup, c.490 BC.

body, pinned on the shoulders, and sometimes tied at the waist with a girdle or belt. It fell towards the feet in quite stiff, heavy folds, and may have been seen as suitable attire for demure young women who were on display in a public procession. The *chiton*, the tunic worn by the married women (see also Fig. 9), seems often to have been made of lighter linen fabric, so that it produced a more rippling effect and tended to cling to the body. For this reason it can be quite a sexy garment, but in the frieze the women wearing this style of dress are modestly enveloped in long cloaks, or *himatia*. The *chiton* also differed from the *peplos* in its design, since back and front were made from two separate rectangles of cloth fastened along the arms with small buttons or metal fastenings.

Fig. 9 An indoor scene in which a seated woman is holding a casket, while her maid carries two perfume-jars. The seated woman is wearing a *chiton*, and the maid a *peplos*. A red-figure *hydria*, or water-jar, c.430 BC.

Deadly dresses

Despite being more alluring, the chiton could be seen as less dangerous than the peplos, because it did away with the need for pins. According to the fifth-century historian Herodotus, the *chiton* had become fashionable about a hundred years before his time, after the Athenians had been disastrously defeated in battle by forces from the nearby island of Aegina. When the sole survivor returned to Athens and brought the bad news to the bereaved, he was greeted by women who were bitterly resentful of the fact that he had escaped the fate suffered by their menfolk.

> They crowded round him, drew out the long pins which they used to fasten their peplos garments, and thrust them into his flesh, each of them shouting as she struck, 'Where is my husband?' So the poor fellow was killed...
>
> (HERODOTUS 5.87)

After this episode Athenian women were forced to change their style of dress and switch from the *peplos* to the *chiton*. Meanwhile in Aegina the victors rubbed salt into Athenian wounds by triumphantly decreeing that in future *peplos* pins would be half as long again as they had been before, and that they would form the main offering made by women at shrines.

One striking feature of this anecdote is the attribution of menacing qualities to a garment which ordinarily seems to have been seen as thoroughly respectable. In our own society a story about a woman wearing a twin-set who used her pearls to garrotte the bearer of a piece of bad news might have a similar impact. This can be thought of as one symptom of a tendency on the part of Greek writers to regard all females, even those who are apparently chaste and virtuous, as potentially threatening to the male sex. If anything, the chaste women are more dangerous, because one is not on one's guard against them. The same pattern of thought can be discerned in stories about the deadly impact of some of the textiles which women manufactured at home, in a society where wool-working was regarded as the prime activity of the dutiful wife and mother. We shall be looking at some of these stories in the next chapter.

Exposure and concealment

It is not at all surprising that women's dangerous qualities were thought of as being exercised through items of clothing. In Classical Athens, even more than in other societies, women were particularly identified with clothes, both because in real life they manufactured most of them and because in Greek art they wore far more of them than men did. In the 500s BC it became conventional for sculptors to represent male figures in the nude, particularly when depicting warriors, heroes, or athletes. The first large-scale statue of an unclothed female, however, did not appear until about 340 BC, towards the end of the classical period. Even in vase-paintings, where artists tended to be more adventurous, female nudes were not particularly common.

The Greek custom of performing athletics naked would to some extent have influenced the popularity of the male nude. Yet men did not appear naked in most of the real-life situations in which they are shown in this condition by artists. They did not, for example, go into battle or take part in religious processions in the nude, so that in this respect the unclothed male riders in the Parthenon frieze are quite unrealistic. In part, the convention of male nudity can be seen as one expression of the Greek ideals of freedom and openness. The absence of concealment being promoted in representations of men's bodies matched the freedom of speech which men cultivated in political and philosophical debate. But women did not possess the same freedoms; they were supposed to be confined to the home, and in a similar manner they were confined inside their clothes by Greek artists. In this way modesty was proclaimed as a desirable attribute of Athenian women, but at the same time the folds of drapery enclosing their forms gave them an air of mystery. An ability to keep things concealed, which in some circumstances can be interpreted as deliberate deceitfulness, was seen as one of the prime characteristics of women.

Women looking at men

In Athens women did not go to athletics shows, and most of them would never have seen any naked men other than their husbands; however they would have come across plenty of statues, some of them quite close to home. Many Athenian houses had objects known as herms outside their doors: these were stone pillars with a head of the god Hermes at the top and a sculpture of an erect penis half way down. The herm's function was to protect the household and bring it prosperity and fertility. It would also have reminded any woman leaving the house that the public space which she was entering was dominated by male values and activities. The woman's place was inside the home.

Naked goddesses

When naked women are shown in paintings on pots they are often (though not always) clearly distinguished as prostitutes. In real life most prostitutes working in low-grade brothels were slaves, and one of the features which helps us to identify female slaves in general is their short hair. So when a naked woman in a painting has short hair we can be fairly safe in assuming that an Athenian viewer would have recognised her as a prostitute, even if she is not actually engaged in sexual activity.

When the female nude finally made an appearance in sculpture, she was rather different from her painted predecessors. The statue which was probably the first large-scale depiction of a naked female in Greek art was produced as late as 340 BC. It was the work of a famous Athenian sculptor called Praxiteles, and it represented the goddess Aphrodite. In its day it created a great sensation. Praxiteles offered it for sale, along with a more conventional clothed statue, to the people of the island of Cos, who opted for the 'sober and decent ' version (PLINY THE ELDER 36.4.20-21). The nude Aphrodite was eventually sold to the Greek city of Knidos, on the west coast of the modern state of Turkey, where it became a great tourist attraction.

There was a popular piece of gossip about a young man who developed a passion for this statue and managed to get locked into Aphrodite's shrine overnight. While there he made love to the marble goddess and left a permanent stain on her. This is one of a number of anecdotes from the Greek world which dwell on the life-like qualities of works of art. The most famous is the story of the sculptor Pygmalion, who fell in love with his own ivory statue of a woman. He used to kiss and fondle it, and bring it presents of flowers, pet birds and jewellery. Eventually Aphrodite took pity on him, and the next time he kissed the statue he felt its body stir beneath his own:

> Then Pygmalion poured out his grateful thanks to the goddess,
> and once again pressed his own lips to lips that were real at last.
> (OVID, *Metamorphoses* 10.290-92)

All ended happily, and Aphrodite herself attended their wedding.

These stories seem rather bizarre to us, though perhaps less so when we remember some of the tales about blow-up dolls which circulate in our own society. More importantly, we have to remember that painting, pottery and sculpture were almost the only visual media which the Greeks possessed, so that having a crush on a statue would have been for them the equivalent of an infatuation with a TV or pop star. Another significant element in these narratives is the way in which they equate women with objects – indeed the statues in these stories might well be referred to as 'sex objects'. As we shall see, the very first female, Pandora, was also regarded as an item which had been manufactured, and therefore as less fully human than her male counterparts.

The statue of Aphrodite which was sold to Knidos no longer exists, but we do have a number of copies of it made by later Roman sculptors

Fig. 10 Statue of Aphrodite. A Roman copy of an original by Praxiteles, from Knidos, c.340 BC.

(Fig. 10). The goddess is shown with a water-jar and towel by her side, and appears to have been disturbed by an unseen intruder while taking a bath. Her head is turned to one side, and she is holding one hand in front of her genital area, as though trying to hide it. So even when depicting Aphrodite the sculptor feels that he has to provide an excuse – the bathing operations – for the female's nudity. This statue is therefore unlike the hundreds of figures of nude heroes and warriors which were produced in ancient Greece, in that here the nudity is not taken for granted. This is a woman who is normally covered up, the sculptor seems to be announcing, but has now been uncovered. Our viewing of her appears to be unauthorised – the goddess does not want to be seen – and for that reason its erotic qualities are heightened.

To us it may seem surprising that any goddess at all should be depicted in the nude, although Aphrodite was certainly the obvious candidate for this kind of daring treatment, since she was the deity most associated with sex. After 340 BC naked Aphrodites became quite common, and their arrival on the scene is indicative of a new and more personal attitude towards divinities, and in general of a new sensuality in Greek art. But Athena and Artemis, both virgin goddesses, were never pictured in this way, even towards the end of the classical period. Their status as unmarried females would have meant that their bodies had to be kept securely hidden from male eyes.

This important social rule is emphasised in a couple of cautionary mythological tales. The one which features Athena relates how a young man called Teiresias once caught sight of the goddess while she was bathing in a spring. Although his glimpse of the naked divinity had been quite involuntary, Teiresias was punished by being struck blind; but he did receive some compensation in the form of the power of prophecy, making him into the most celebrated seer of Greek mythology. This story gives a graphic demonstration of the danger which men encounter when they engage in any kind of sexual contact with unmarried virgins, even if it is limited to gazing at their nudity.

In the other story an accidental glimpse of a naked goddess provoked an even more disastrous punishment. When a hunter named Actaeon came across Artemis taking a skinny dip in a woodland pool he was changed into a stag, and then his own hounds rounded on him and tore him to pieces. Again the dangers of consorting with virgins are highlighted. This tale probably carries an additional message, about the importance of conserving one's energy when engaged in strenuous activities like hunting, and not using it up in erotic encounters. Actaeon, though unwittingly, failed to follow this rule, and so he lost the battle which every hunter wages against the animal kingdom.

Among the Greeks there was a widespread belief that when they were involved in outdoor pursuits men ought to abstain from sexual activity, because contact with women was bound to weaken them. This was probably one of the reasons why athletes taking part in the Olympic games had to give up sex for thirty days before the contests began; similar unofficial sanctions exist in our own society when men are participating in major sporting events such as the World Cup. As the patron deity of hunters, the virgin goddess Artemis was an excellent advertisement for this kind of embargo: she promised men success in the hunt, but was herself sexually unavailable.

Puberty, and a warning about wells

The philosopher Aristotle tells us that in his day – the fourth century BC – girls' breasts began to swell and they started to menstruate at about the age of thirteen (ARISTOTLE, *History of animals* 581 a-b). We have little information about the practical aspects of menstruation, but it seems that women used woollen rags as sanitary towels, probably pieces of material which were left over after garments had been made. In general, male writers tend to see a woman's periods as the cause of numerous medical difficulties. Young unmarried women who are not having sexual intercourse are seen as being particularly prone to these: their blood does not flow so easily, either because it is not being heated by intercourse, or because the mouth of the womb has not yet been opened up. This in turn may lead to grave psychological problems. The anonymous author of one medical treatise tells us that at the onset of puberty girls are liable to suffer from hallucinations, brought on when their menstrual blood does not flow out of their bodies but rushes up to their heart and lungs. They become feverish and sometimes suicidally insane; some of them have visions which encourage them to throw themselves down wells and drown themselves. But according to this particular writer the remedy is a relatively straightforward one:

> My prescription is that when virgins have this trouble they should marry as soon as possible. If they become pregnant they will be cured.
>
> *(On Virgins)*

Stories such as these about the perils of puberty are very much in line with the prevailing notion, mentioned above, that adolescent girls are prone to wildness, and may even become deranged. The lesson to be drawn from this particular stereotype is always the same – girls should be married off as soon as possible after puberty. Medical writers are able to supply a good physiological reason for this, and one moreover that seems to have the woman's best interests at heart: 'if women have intercourse with men their health is better than if they do not' (*On the Seed* 4). In fact, marriage, sex and motherhood were seen as the only long-term roles available to a woman, so that the sooner she settled down to them, it was believed, the more comfortable life would be for all concerned.

Phrasikleia: a woman who died before she was married

Most women seem to have been married between the ages of fourteen and eighteen. The fact that girls were thought of as wild and difficult to control would have been one reason for early matrimony, especially since the girls' fathers, generally aged at least forty-five by this time, would have wanted to get their daughters settled before they died. It was also terribly important that unmarried women should not get pregnant, and the easiest way of guarding against this was to provide them with husbands as soon as possible. Wanting women to have a large number of children was probably not a factor – during this period most Athenians seem to have been keen to limit the size of their families.

If a young woman died before she was married, it was thought that she had been prevented from achieving her true goal in life. Sometimes a special kind of pottery jar called a *loutrophoros* or 'purification-jug', which was normally used to give a bride her ritual bath on the eve of her wedding, was placed on her tomb (Fig. 11, p. 26). This indicated that instead of becoming an ordinary bride, the young woman had been married to Death.

This is the epitaph of one Athenian woman named Phrasikleia:

> I shall be called a maiden for ever. I have been granted this name
> by the gods in place of a wedding.

Pandora: garments, gifts and the deceitfulness of women

An early Greek poet named Hesiod, writing in about 700 BC, has provided us with two versions of the story of Pandora, who in myth was the first human female. As such, she was the Greek equivalent of the biblical Eve. The two versions share the same basic plot. Zeus, the ruler of the gods, refused to allow mortals the use of fire, but a minor deity called Prometheus stole a burning brand from Mount Olympus and carried it down to earth. Zeus was furious and punished Prometheus by chaining him to a rock, where an eagle gnawed at his liver. The human race, which at this stage consisted entirely of men, was punished in a

Fig. 11 Mourning women at a funeral. Their raised arms indicate that they are tearing their hair, and in the lower scene they are standing round the corpse. A black-figure *loutrophoros*, c.500 BC.

more subtle fashion, when Zeus masterminded the creation of the first woman. He ordered the craftsman god Hephaistos to mould an image of a young virgin out of clay. On this level, then, Pandora resembled some of the other sculpted sex objects which we have already encountered.

A number of deities then presented the new arrival with gifts: Athena gave her a silvery dress and a veil, and taught her how to weave; Aphrodite gave her charm and desire, the Graces some golden necklaces, and the Seasons a crown of spring flowers. In one version of the story

Hermes, the god of eloquence and trickery, gave her a voice, and to go with it 'the morals of a bitch' and 'lies, and wheedling words, and a cunning nature' (HESIOD, *Works and Days* 67 and 78). The Greek word 'Pandora' means 'Allgifts'. Not only does Pandora receive presents from various divinities, she herself is seen as a gift, which the race of men foolishly accepts from the gods because they are deceived by the woman's superficial attractions. Like many a free gift, Pandora is not all that she is made out to be. According to Hesiod, her lovely exterior conceals a vicious and exploitative nature, which she hands down to all her female descendants,

That deadly female race and tribe of wives
Who live with mortal men and cause great harm,
No companions to men in their poverty, only in wealth.

(HESIOD, *Theogony* 590-593)

So the deceptive character of gifts is one of the prominent themes of the Pandora story. In ancient Greece the exchange of gifts was an important social ritual which helped to solemnise the establishment of friendly relations with another person or community. But social relationships could be tricky, and so too, on occasions, were the presents which accompanied them. In myth the most famous example of a fraudulent gift is the wooden horse which the Greeks left as an offering outside the walls of Troy, crammed with soldiers who would quickly destroy the city. A woman was also seen as a kind of gift, for still in fifth-century Athens the exchange of women in marriage was an important way of creating a relationship with another family, or *oikos*. Pandora reminds us that this gift too might be deceptive – as with the Trojan horse its exterior might conceal a dangerous inner space. Among Greek men there seems to have been an ever-present fear that their wives might be deceiving them when they presented them with the contents of their wombs, or inner compartments.

In one of the versions of the Pandora story the woman's dangerous interior is represented in symbolic form, by a jar (Pandora's box was a later invention). Up till now men had lived free from sorrow, disease and the need for hard work; but when the first woman lifted the lid from her jar, all the pains and evils hidden inside flew out:

Only hope remained inside the jar's thick walls
Beneath its rim, and did not fly through the door.
For the lid of the jar stopped it.

But thousands of troubles drifted off among mortals.
For the earth is full of evils, and the sea.

(HESIOD, *Works and days* 96-101)

But a woman's interior can also produce good gifts, the children that a man needs if he is to have someone to look after him in his old age and inherit his property when he dies. So woman herself is a double-edged gift, and it seems that men have little alternative but to accept her.

The view of women conjured up by these Pandora stories is so jaundiced that it comes as rather a surprise to learn that a scene showing the creation of the first female was depicted on the base of the great statue of Athena inside the Parthenon. There is some evidence to suggest that in Athens Pandora was sometimes worshipped as a goddess of fertility, so the Athenian men who gazed at the statue may have been more conscious than we imagine of the positive aspects of womanhood. However, Hesiod's rendering of the Pandora story was so famous that it is hard to believe that they would not also have remembered what to them was the downside of femininity – women's ability to trap and deceive men.

Chapter 3
Married women

New husbands, new homes

For the married women in the Parthenon frieze the Panathenaic procession would have been a reminder of an earlier and more personal event, when as brides they were led in procession to the homes of their new husbands. Marriage was the most significant social transition which a woman ever underwent, and for her it must have been quite a daunting, not to say frightening, experience. One young woman, in a fragment of a lost play by Sophocles, gives us a flavour of the feelings with which some girls would have anticipated their weddings:

> It is my belief that young women in their fathers' homes lead the sweetest lives of all. For ignorance always keeps children secure and happy. But when we reach womanhood and gain some understanding, we are thrust out and sold away from our ancestral gods and our parents. Some go to live with strangers, some with foreigners, some go to joyless homes, some to unfriendly ones. All these things, once a single night has yoked us to our husbands, we are obliged to praise, and consider a happy outcome.
>
> (SOPHOCLES, fragment 524)

A new husband might with good reason have been viewed by some brides as a stranger, for all marriages were arranged by the groom and the young woman's father or guardian. As far as we know the woman was not even given a say in the choice of her husband. In some cases she would scarcely have known the man she was marrying, while in others she would at least have met him a few times, since marriages between first cousins were relatively common. For the bride marriage involved some fundamental changes – a move to a new home, the loss of her virginity, and the prospect of sharing her life with a man who was generally much older than she was, about thirty as compared to her fourteen to eighteen. For some of the women living in the rural communities of Athens marriage also meant a move to another village or town, which might be some distance from her parents' home. To a young woman who had only recently reached puberty all these changes may have seemed rather terrifying; and it is little wonder that, as we shall see, some of the rituals which surrounded marriage spoke more of grief than of joy.

When a woman was married she passed from the guardianship of her father into that of her husband. Legally, an Athenian female remained a minor for the whole of her life – she was always assumed to be under the protection of a male guardian, or *kyrios*, who was responsible for her financial support, and acted as her representative in all matters with a legal significance. If her husband died, then her eldest son took over the role of *kyrios*, provided he was aged eighteen or over. Otherwise she returned to the guardianship of her father, or male next-of-kin (her brother, uncle or cousin).

Aristotle's daughter

Arrangements for a daughter's marriage could be made even if her father died when she was still a small girl. One of the clauses in the will of the philosopher Aristotle states:

> When my daughter is grown up, she should be given in marriage to Nikanor.... If anything should happen to Nikanor (which heaven forbid), either before he marries my daughter, or when he has married her but before there are children, any arrangements he shall make shall be valid. If Theophrastos is willing to take my daughter in marriage, he shall have the same rights as Nikanor. If not, the executors in consultation with Antipater shall administer with regards to my daughter...as seems best to them.
>
> (DIOGENES LAERTIUS 5.12-13)

Wedding ceremonies

A wedding was marked by a number of rituals. Shortly before the event, at a betrothal ceremony called *engue*, the bride-to-be's father or guardian pronounced the words, 'I hand over this woman to you for the ploughing of legitimate children'. This formula made use of a common metaphor, comparing a woman to a piece of land. It called to mind both the fertility of the female and her husband's territorial control over it.

On the evening of the wedding itself a feast was held in the house of the bride's father. Then at nightfall the bride and groom were transported to their new home in a càrt or a chariot, accompanied by a retinue of relatives and friends (Fig. 12). On their arrival they were greeted by the

Fig. 12 A wedding procession. A red-figure pyxis, or cosmetics-jar, c.440 BC.

groom's mother, who was carrying torches symbolic of the rekindling of the family line which the marriage would ensure. The bride was led into the house by her husband and conducted to the hearth, the focal point of her new home. The guests called out that the bride and groom were 'Blessed!' and showered the couple with nuts and dried fruits, signifying prosperity and fertility. The climax of the proceedings came when the bride was led by the groom towards the bedroom, while the guests sang a wedding hymn. It was probably at this stage that the bride removed her veil with a formal gesture. Inside the bedroom there were two final rituals before the marriage was consummated: the bride ate a quince, an emblem of her sexuality, and the groom removed her belt or girdle.

Alcestis' wedding

In the tragedy *Alcestis*, by Euripides, the heroine's husband Admetos laments his wife's recent death by recalling the former happiness of their wedding procession:

> How terrible the change!
> Then, with pine torches from Pelion,
> With wedding-songs I marched inside,
> Holding aloft the hand of my darling wife.
> Revellers followed shouting out loud, calling
> Down blessings on Alcestis, now dead, and myself.
> Two old and noble families, they said,
> Were being joined together in our marriage.
> Now a dirge has stifled the wedding-song;
> Black robes have replaced our white gowns.
>
> (EURIPIDES, *Alcestis* 913-23)

Processions of all kinds: festivals, weddings and funerals

Any procession is a form of public display in which a group of people exhibits its unity and strength both to itself and to the outside world. Because it is mobile the procession also links together two or more different locations and emphasises the group's relationship to those places. The great Panathenaic celebration depicted in the Parthenon frieze illustrates both of these features. It included representatives of various sections of Athenian society – young warriors, older males, women (Fig. 5, p. 9), resident aliens, and so on – and by bringing these sections together within the orderly framework of the procession it provided a demonstration of the solidarity fostered by the *polis* of Athens. The procession, then, can be seen as a kind of microcosm of the *polis,* given added significance and permanence when it was included in the sculptural decoration of the city's most prominent temple. In real life the Panathenaic procession made its way from the main gate of the city to its sacred centre, the Acropolis; and so by its movements it created a link between the city's walls, the physical guarantee of its security, and its religious and emotional core.

Of course, the view of Athens being presented in the Parthenon frieze was an idealised one, and far from complete. Slaves, for example, were not included in the picture. This makes it all the more significant that women, though certainly far fewer in number than their male companions, were awarded a prominent position in both the procession and the frieze. Athenian females were undoubtedly subservient to men, but the important role which they played in the *polis* was being publicly acknowledged when they were given a place in these important spectacles.

Women would have participated in a number of other religious processions, such as the one which walked fourteen miles along the Sacred Way from Athens to Eleusis, to celebrate the Mysteries of Demeter – which will be discussed in the next section. Apart from these there were two other occasions when it was considered important to display a woman to the outside world in this way. One was the wedding procession, and the other the retinue which escorted a woman's corpse to the cemetery.

In the wedding procession it was the uniting of two families through the transfer of a woman from one home to another which was being advertised. This ceremony was considered so important that it was the feature of the wedding most frequently depicted by vase-painters. The scene in Fig. 12 is a 'stretched-out' version of a painting in the British Museum which decorates a round cosmetics-jar known as a *pyxis.* On the jar the procession is actually moving around in a circle, so that the door on the left is both its starting-point and its destination.This door symbolises not just one but two family homes, which are being brought together by this marriage. The Athenians believed that links of this kind were a very important source of unity in the *polis.* They were reinforced by the transfer of property which accompanied the transfer of the bride. In the painting the wedding-gifts carried by the women on the left are a reminder of a much more substantial item of property, the dowry, which a bride took with her into her new family.

Family traditions as well as solidarity were being exhibited in the funeral procession, which established a physical link between a family's home and the cemetery where its ancestors were buried. When they died women were apparently given as elaborate a send-off as their menfolk. Corpses were bathed, anointed with oil, and dressed in linen with a wreath on the head, before being laid on a bier and displayed to the mourners. Although men came to look at the body, the chief role in mourning was played by the women of the family, who gathered round the bier tearing their hair, striking their breasts, and singing laments (Fig. 11, p. 26). These emotional peformances were very much a part of the ritual, and it is difficult to say how much genuine feeling they involved. On the next day the body was carried to the cemetery on a cart, followed by a procession of relatives. It was either buried as it was, or burned and the ashes placed in the ground in an urn. So a married woman's existence, spent to a large extent within the private space of the home, was framed by two public journeys, one of them joining her to a new household and the other to the company of that household's dead.

Marriage, abduction and ritual death. The bride as Persephone

It has often been pointed out that the ceremonial treatment of a corpse described in the last section was very similar to the treatment received by a bride. Both involved a ritual bath, adornment in special clothes and a wreath of leaves, and a procession to a new home. The similarity was certainly noticed by ancient writers, for there are many allusions to it in tragedy. In Sophocles' *Antigone*, for example, when the unmarried heroine is led off in procession to the underground cavern in which she is to die, she cries out, 'Oh tomb, oh bridal chamber!' (SOPHOCLES, *Antigone* 891).

The comparison certainly emphasises the passive role assigned to a bride, who was transported from one place to another as though she were indeed a corpse. It also brings to mind the grief and sense of loss which the girl's family experienced when she was married. This reluctance to let her go may have been ritually demonstrated by other ceremonies. At the start of the procession the groom picked the bride up and placed her in the cart, and at their destination he led her indoors with her wrist clasped in his hand, a sign of his power over his wife. These features may represent an acting out of a kind of abduction, the forcible removal of the bride from her family. In a society in which hunting was still regarded as a typical male activity marriage was sometimes likened to a young man's successful pursuit of his prey – girls, we remember, were often compared to animals.

In myth the ultimate example of the corpse-like bride is provided by Persephone, daughter of Demeter, the goddess of corn and cultivation. One day while she was picking flowers, Persephone was snatched up by

Hades, the ruler of the dead, and carried off to be his bride in the Underworld. Persephone's marriage, then, was preceded by an abduction or rape, and she became the wife of Death himself. This had all been arranged by the girl's father, Zeus, without the knowledge of her mother. For nine days Demeter wandered the earth searching for her daughter, with a blazing torch in either hand. When she finally discovered what had happened to Persephone she was so furious that she refused to allow the crops to grow:

> She said she would never set foot on fragrant Olympus,
> Never allow the crops to sprout out of the earth,
> Till she had seen with her own eyes her lovely-faced daughter.
> (*Homeric Hymn to Demeter* 331-3)

These strike tactics had their effect and Zeus eventually relented, sending the god Hermes off to the Underworld to bring Persephone back. But before she left, Hades gave her a pomegranate seed to eat and this simple meal established an unbreakable bond between husband and wife. When Persephone was taken up into the light of day, she and her mother rushed joyfully into each other's arms. But the anxious Demeter immediately asked, 'My child, when you were down below, did you perhaps eat any food?' (*Homeric Hymn to Demeter* 393-4). If she did, Demeter explained, she would be bound to spend a third of every year in the Underworld, returning to her mother for the remaining two-thirds. This was how things turned out. Every year in the spring-time, when Persephone rose out of the ground, her mother Demeter allowed the crops to grow and life to revive (Fig. 13, p. 36).

The story of Persephone and Demeter was acted out every September as part of a secret set of rituals known as the Eleusinian Mysteries. These were celebrated in Eleusis, the town where in the myth the mother and daughter had been reunited, which was fourteen miles to the west of the city of Athens. Both males and females could be initiated into the Mysteries, and we can easily imagine that for women the performance of the myth would have been a reminder of some of the negative aspects of marriage. Indeed, marriage to Death would in itself have been a very real fear, for in ancient Greece many women died in childbirth. However, the main impact of the rites lay in their celebration of the rebirth of the crops and the renewal of human life, and women would doubtless have derived some consolation from the knowledge that they were intimately involved in both these processes.

Fig. 13 Persephone and Demeter, standing on either side of a young man named Triptolemos, who is seated in a winged chariot. Persephone is holding some corn and a torch, while Demeter carries a torch and pours a drink-offering into the bowl held by Triptolemos. After she had been reunited with her daughter, Demeter taught the art of agriculture to Triptolemos, and sent him off round the world to pass on this skill to the rest of the human race. Triptolemos is also holding some stalks of corn. A red-figure cup, c.480 BC.

The lifting of the veil

In Athens veils were of two main types. A woman could either drape her cloak or *himation* over her head in order to form a veil (Fig. 12, p. 31); or she used a separate piece of material, like a large scarf, which again was worn loosely over the head (Fig. 14). The evidence is very limited, but it seems that veils were used mainly when women went out of the house or appeared in the company of males to whom they were not related; and sometimes as well as covering their heads they also held the veil up in front of their faces, so that only their eyes could be seen. But there may not have been any hard and fast rules about when veils were necessary; for instance, most of the women in the Parthenon frieze are wearing cloaks, but none of them is veiled, even though as participants in the Panathenaic procession they would have been very much in the public eye.

There were certain occasions, however, when veils were evidently a ritual requirement. Although men were not usually required to cover their

Fig. 14 Tombstone of a woman named Hegeso. Hegeso's elegant clothes and chair indicate that she came from a wealthy family. She is being handed a jewel-box by her slave-girl, the figure on the left. From the cemetery at Athens, c.400 BC.

heads, both sexes veiled themselves when they were mourning dead relatives and here the gesture can be understood as an effort to maintain the privacy of very powerful emotions. For women the most significant occasion when the veil was used was certainly her marriage. In vase paintings showing wedding processions, like the one in Fig. 12 (p. 31), the bride is wearing her veil draped over her head. It was probably when she reached her new home that she performed the ritual gesture of unveiling, or *anakalypteria*. This can be partly explained as a demonstration of her transition to a new status. When she hid herself inside her veil before leaving her old home she became a sort of non-person; the later removal of the veil signified that she had been reborn as a married woman. Actions with this meaning are quite common in rites of passage, the ceremonies which accompany the entry into a new stage of life.

The unveiling gesture was also linked to a woman's *aidos* – her modesty, or shyness with men. Her voluntary removal of the veil in the presence of her husband reminded the onlookers that this was an exceptional circumstance, and that in the company of other men her head would remain demurely covered. This impression of modesty, coupled with humility, would have been reinforced by the woman's downcast eyes; but at the same time the unveiling announced that the bride was prepared to expose her body to her husband, so that it served as symbolic prelude to their sexual relationship. The dual meaning of the gesture would have captured perfectly the ambivalent character of the role given to an Athenian wife, who was valued for her sexuality, but strictly limited in the extent to which she could exercise it.

Because it was so much associated with weddings, the unveiling gesture was used in art to denote not just a bride, but also a wife. One of the most famous examples can be seen in the Parthenon frieze, where Hera is represented sitting next to her husband Zeus and holding out her veil (Fig. 15). Her pose tells us that she is married to the male by her side; but with Hera it has an added significance, since she was worshipped in many parts of the Greek world as the goddess of marriage.

Gyges and the wife of the king of Lydia

The relationship between a woman's *aidos* and her clothing is dramatically illustrated in the story of Gyges, told by the historian Herodotus (1.8-13). Candaules was the king of Lydia in Asia Minor, and he was so proud of his wife's beauty that he invited his favourite bodyguard, Gyges, to look at her when she was naked. Gyges was horrified, and protested that 'when a woman sheds her *chiton*, she sheds her *aidos*'.

The king eventually managed to overcome Gyges' objections, and arranged for him to hide behind the open door of the royal bedroom when the queen was undressing for bed:

> As she was laying aside her garments Gyges looked at her. Then, when she turned her back on him and got into bed, he slipped secretly out of the room. But the king's wife caught sight of him as he was leaving.
>
> (HERODOTUS 1.10)

Fig. 15 Part of the east section of the Parthenon frieze: slab V, c.440 BC. From left to right: Nike (the goddess of victory) or Iris (female messenger of the gods); Hera, holding out her veil; her husband Zeus.

Realising that her husband was to blame for this outrage, the queen prevented herself from calling out. Next morning she summoned the servant and presented him with two choices. He could either kill Candaules, seize the throne, and marry her; or he could prepare to die on the spot. Gyges sensibly chose the first course of action. That night he stabbed the king to death as he slept, and so became the new ruler. He had witnessed a spectacle which only a husband ought to have seen – a wife's removal of her clothes and her *aidos*; and to blot out the shame of this he had either to die or to become her legitimate spouse.

The bride's dowry. 'First we women have to pay out a huge sum of money to purchase a husband.'

When the tragic heroine Medea uses these words in her passionate outpouring on the wrongs of women (EURIPIDES, *Medea* 232-3), she is exaggerating: the dowry was in fact paid by the bride's father. It was usually a sum of money, although other property such as jewellery or household goods might be included. Yet Medea did have a point. The dowry represented a daughter's share in the family inheritance, received on marriage rather than on her father's death. So though the money technically belonged to her, it was handed over to her husband and passed immediately into his control. In theory it was possible for a woman to marry without a dowry, but in practice great moral pressure was placed even on poor men to produce a sum of money for their daughters. 'Who would ever have taken a dowerless wife from a penniless man ...?' is the woeful plea made on behalf of one hard-up father desperately seeking a spouse for his child (DEMOSTHENES 59.8).

As was the case in Britain after the First World War, these worries became very pressing during a period when a major war had deprived the community of many of its menfolk. In the famous comedy *Lysistrata,* written by Aristophanes during the Peloponnesian War, the enterprising heroine who gives the play its title calls the women of Athens out on a sex-strike in order to persuade the men of the city to make peace with the Spartans. One of Lysistrata's grievances is this problem of finding husbands in wartime conditions:

> About our own plight I will say no more.
> But I grieve for the unmarried women who
> are growing old in their bridal chambers.
> (ARISTOPHANES, *Lysistrata* 592-3)

Once a husband had been found and the marriage arranged, the dowry was handed over: in normal circumstances it was the only substantial piece of property ever owned by a woman. Farming land, the source of most people's livelihood, was passed on to a man's son or sons. If he had no sons, but did have a daughter, she still could not inherit his estate. Instead, when he died, she was married off to his male next-of-kin, who took control of the family property until his own son – the dead man's grandson – became old enough to inherit. This happened even when the next-of-kin was the daughter's uncle, for such marriages were not considered incestuous in Athens.

Even when a wife was allowed access to the dowry, she was only able to spend it in small amounts. Women were prevented by law from making any purchases which cost more than the price of a few basic household provisions. A husband on the other hand did have the right to spend the dowry, and he may not even have needed to consult his wife. Most dowries of a reasonable size were probably invested in land. A sensible husband would not have used the money to go on extravagant shopping sprees, since on divorce the total amount had to be returned to the woman's father. Failure to do this meant that interest had to be paid at the very high rate of 18% per year. So the dowry can be seen as something which might deter a husband from divorcing his wife for frivolous reasons; in addition a threat from the woman's family to initiate a divorce and take back the dowry might be enough to prevent a man from ill-treating his wife. Domestic violence certainly occurred in Athens: when Lysistrata, for instance, dares to criticise the way in which men are handling the Peloponnesian War, her husband responds by bawling, 'Back to your weaving woman, or you'll be nursing a black eye for the rest of the week' (ARISTOPHANES, *Lysistrata* 519-20).

The dowry, then, gave a woman a degree of protection and possibly even some power within the marriage. According to Plato *(Laws* 774c), the existence of this fund of money made wives bossy and husbands subservient. But some men were certainly skinflints when it came to spending the income from a large dowry on their spouses. This is one author's description of a tight-fisted husband's treatment of his wife:

> His wife brought him a talent in dowry, and has borne him a son. But since then he's only ever given her a couple of coppers for treats, and even on holidays he makes her wash in cold water.
>
> (THEOPHRASTUS, *Characters* 28.4)

The importance of producing a son

To an Athenian male the fact that the skinflint's wife had borne him a son made his behaviour seem particularly mean. Giving birth to a boy (Fig. 16, p. 42) was the greatest service which a wife could perform for her husband, since this meant that his family or *oikos* would be perpetuated, and also that there would be someone to inherit the family farm. This was an important consideration not only for most individual Athenians but also for the Athenian state as a whole. One way of guarding against civil unrest in a community was to try to guarantee that most families had enough to live on, and that wealth did not become concentrated in too few hands. Thus it was important that landed property was transmitted smoothly from one generation of a family to the next, and did not pass into the ownership of a few wealthy men. Athenian women, by giving birth to sons, made a vital contribution to this process.

Fig. 16 A domestic interior. The man on the right looks at his seated wife, who is handing her baby boy to a nurse. Behind the nurse there is a loom. Textiles and babies were considered to be the two most important products produced by Athenian women. A red-figure *hydria*, or water-jar, c.430 BC.

In addition, an Athenian son when he reached the age of eighteen would assume the political privileges and obligations of a citizen, and would be able to participate in the government of Athens. So women were involved in the transmission of power as well as of property. Their part in this process was recognised in 451 BC, when the statesman Pericles introduced a law which stipulated that in order to qualify as a citizen a man had to be of Athenian parentage on both sides, and not just on that of his father, as had previously been the case. This law may have been introduced in order to deter Athenian men from acquiring non-Athenian wives. Many Greeks from other states had settled in Athens to take advantage of its employment opportunities, and there may well have been a fear that men would begin to marry the daughters of these immigrants, making it more difficult for local women to find husbands. One of the effects of the law would certainly have been to enhance the status of Athenian-born women by placing added emphasis on their role in the social system. The downside of this would have been that the pressure placed on them to produce legitimate sons was increased.

The political importance of women's child-bearing function is highlighted in some simple words spoken by the female chorus in *Lysistrata*:

'I have a share in public service. For I contribute men.'

(ARISTOPHANES, *Lysistrata* 651)

Few members of the audience would have failed to appreciate the significance of this statement. The play was performed not long after a disastrous military expedition to Sicily, when thousands of Athenians had lost their lives. The city was still at this time desperately short of soldiers.

Later on in this chapter we will be looking at the measures which the Athenians introduced to try to ensure the legitimacy of their sons. But what happened if a woman was unable to conceive a child in the first place? If Aristophanes is to be believed, a lively black-market in male babies existed in Athens. This is one character's description of how it operated:

I knew a woman once who was in labour for ten whole days. That's how long it took to find a baby she could buy. Her husband was rushing around purchasing drugs to speed up the birth. Then the old midwife fetched the baby indoors in a big stew-pot, with a honeycomb bunged in its mouth to stop it from howling. When the old woman gave her the nod the poor suffering wife started shouting, 'Get out, get out, husband, I'm about to give birth.' For the little brat was already trying to kick its way out of the pot. Husband's delighted. Dashes out of the room. Wife pulls the plug out of the baby's mouth. Baby cries. The rascally old woman (the one that brought the baby) rushes out beaming. 'It's a boy, a real lion of a boy. He's the image of you, every last detail, right down to his little willy. It's got a kink at the end, just like yours.' Aren't these the kind of tricks we get up to? By Artemis, they are.

(ARISTOPHANES, *Women celebrating the Thesmophoria* 502-16)

A male playwright who specialises in comic fantasy is probably not the most reliable of informants where women's secret stratagems are concerned. But in Classical Athens the pressure on wives to produce sons was so great that it seems quite likely that they would sometimes have resorted to ruses like this one.

On a more conventional level, Greek medical writers recommend a wide variety of treatments for infertility. These consist of potions, ointments, fumigations, or pessaries. For instance, one prescription involves the insertion of a woollen pessary which had been dipped in a mixture of ox marrow, goose fat, rose oil, and the root of a plant called thapsia. This was to be left in the body for four days, and in the meantime the woman was to drink a potion made of leek juice and white wine (*On superfetation* 32-3). Remedies such as these can have had very little effect, and it is not surprising that women often turned to higher powers in their efforts to conceive. Asklepios, the god of medicine, was one of the deities most frequently consulted. His sanctuary at Epidauros specialised in 'dream cures', in the course of which sick people slept in a dormitory near to the temple and had dreams which, hopefully, restored them to health. In the inscriptions set up to record these cures many cases of infertility are mentioned. This is one example:

Andromache, from Epirus, for offspring. In her sleep here she had a dream. She dreamt that a lovely young boy uncovered her, and then the god touched her with his hand. After that Andromache bore a son to Arybbas.

Treatments for infertility, whether human or divine, were always aimed at women. Would-be fathers were never seen as needing medical intervention, in spite of a theory held in some quarters that the dominant role in conception was played by the male. The most notorious example of this assertion occurs in the final play of Aeschylus' *Oresteia* trilogy, in a scene in which Orestes is on trial for the murder of his mother, Clytemnestra, who had slaughtered her husband Agamemnon when he returned from the Trojan War. The god Apollo, who had earlier commanded Orestes to avenge his father by killing his mother, now defends him by arguing that his offence was less serious than the one committed by Clytemnestra. She had killed a husband and a father, while Orestes had killed a mother, who is not the true parent of the child:

> For the so-called mother of the child
> is not the real parent, just a nurse to the newly-sown seed.
> The man is the true source of life – the one who mounts.
> She, like a stranger for a stranger, protects
> the young plant, provided a god does not hurt it.
>
> (AESCHYLUS, Eumenides 658-61)

This notion of a mother as a mere vessel for carrying a child was shared by other Greeks, but it was probably not the most common theory of reproduction being put forward at this time. Although the existence of the ovaries had not yet been discovered, a number of scientific writers subscribed to the reasonably accurate belief that the mother as well as the father contributed 'seed' to the embryo.

The 'one-sex' model of the human body

It is a wise child that knows its own father, the saying goes. Only in recent years have tests been developed which can prove the paternity of a child beyond doubt. In ancient Athens there could be no such certainty. But a law against adultery did help to reduce the chances of children and fathers being mistaken about each other's identity; while on a more general cultural level the dominance of the father within the family unit was promoted by pronouncements like the one made by Apollo quoted in the last section. Ideas about human physiology served much the same purpose. In spite of the fact that temperamentally and socially women and men were seen as belonging to entirely different categories, there was nevertheless a tendency among writers on biology to propose what has been referred to as the 'one-sex' model of the human body. Physically the two sexes were not thought of as being complete opposites. Instead, according to Aristotle, 'a woman is, as it were, an infertile male. She is female, in fact, on account of a kind of inequacy' (ARISTOTLE, *Generation of animals* 728a).

So for Aristotle there is really only one sex; fundamentally women are no different from men, but they are constitutionally inferior. In line with this notion of the male body as the model of perfection, he tells us that menstrual blood is the same sort of substance as semen, but it is less pure and concentrated. In the creation of a child, then, the female provides passive matter, while the active life force comes from the male. This view of conception is not exactly the same as the one being presented by Apollo, but once again it underlines the primacy of the father in the parent-child relationship.

The wandering womb

Whatever its precise nature, the part played by the female in reproduction was obviously vital, and tremendous emphasis was placed on it. In the last chapter we looked at some of the medical theories which helped to foster the idea that marriage and childbearing were the proper destiny of a woman. One more diagnosis, remarkable for its eccentricity, deserves to be mentioned here. According to Plato, a woman's womb is a sort of animal, which has a powerful desire to give birth. If this desire is not satisfied, the womb becomes restless and starts to wander around the body, causing all kinds of illnesses. These internal rambles will continue until the woman has sex and becomes pregnant, at which point the womb settles down (PLATO, *Timaios* 91).

Some of the medical writers provide a 'scientific' explanation of this bizarre disorder. If a woman is not having intercourse, they say, her womb is liable to become dry and light, and is easily dislodged. Various itineraries are described. The womb may move towards the head, causing suffocation and foaming at the mouth, or towards the upper abdomen, which brings on drowsiness and loss of voice (*On the diseases of women* 2.123, 126). Sex and pregnancy are the most effective cures, but the writers also recommend a number of interim treatments, involving pessaries, potions, and hot and cold baths. One author even advises the doctor to push the womb back into place with his hands, and then to tie a bandage under the patient's ribs to stop it taking off again.

'If I had to, I'd walk through fire. Anything rather than give up sex.'

Athenian citizens were generally anxious to stress the modesty and decorum of their own wives and daughters, since these qualities helped to guarantee the legitimacy of their children and grandchildren. Yet there was also a strong tendency on the part of Greek men to see women in general (that is, the wives and daughters of other people) as sexually voracious. When the heroine of the comedy *Lysistrata* tries to persuade the other Athenian women to take part in a sex-strike, she is greeted at first with a horrified refusal. One of the women declares that she would rather walk through fire than give up sex:

Lysistrata dear, there's nothing like it.
LYSISTRATA: And what about you?
MYRRHINE: I'd rather walk through fire too.
LYSISTRATA: Oh women, women. We're a hopeless bunch of
tosspots. No wonder they make tragedies out of us...Lampito,
my friend, what about it? Won't you vote for my plan?
LAMPITO: Oh, God. It's hard for a woman to sleep alone at night,
with no little playmate. But we must do it.

(ARISTOPHANES, *Lysistrata* 135-44)

This belief in women's insatiable appetite for sex was linked to the view
that females were somehow closer to nature than males, and therefore
prone to wildness. Unlike men, they were incapable of self-control, or
sophrosune. So if women were unable to keep their lusts in check
themselves, the thinking was, then men would have to do it for them,
through laws and customs which curtailed their freedom. Men had made
themselves into the guardians of women's chastity, and the successful
fulfilment of this role became part of the masculine code of honour.

The image of the randy female was just was one of the ploys used by
Athenian men to assert their moral superiority over women, and to justify
their social dominance. It also enabled them to emphasise the sexual
nature of women's role within the family. Vase-paintings produced towards
the end of the fifth century seem to have served a similar purpose. It
became common to depict brides in particular in what are known as
'boudoir' scenes; they are shown in the women's quarters, arrayed in
jewellery and flimsy dresses, and surrounded by flowers, mirrors and
trinket-boxes. Many of these sensual treatments of the female figure are
found on pots which were used almost exclusively by women, such as
cosmetics or perfume jars. In these paintings women were being invited
to see themselves as sexual beings within an erotic environment; but they
were also reminded that the exercise of this aspect of their identity was
to be strictly confined to the marital bedroom.

This perspective on the role of a wife is rather more inspiring than the
one presented in the famous pronouncement that 'We have prostitutes
for pleasure, mistresses to satisfy the everyday needs of the body, and
wives to bear us legitimate children and be the loyal caretakers of our
homes.' (DEMOSTHENES 59.122). The speaker who made this claim in a
law-court speech would probably not have denied that sexual pleasure
could be an element in marriage; but his words do indicate that Athenian
men took a practical view of the purpose of matrimony, and that neither

romantic love nor close companionship were strongly associated with it. Although Athenian poets and dramatists certainly talk about love, it is rarely seen as a prelude to marriage. This down-to-earth attitude is perhaps to be expected in a society in which arranged marriages were the general rule. It would not necessarily have prevented a loving relationship from developing between husband and wife in the course of the marriage. If marital sex had not sometimes been highly enjoyable, then a scene in *Lysistrata* in which a severely frustrated husband tries to persuade his wife to come to bed with him would hardly have been convincing. The husband, Kinesias, has arrived at the Acropolis to plead with his wife Myrrhine to desert the women's sex-strike. Though she is sorely tempted, Myrrhine remains loyal to her fellow strikers, but she decides to lead her husband on by pretending to be ready for sex. She brings out a camp bed, but just as they are settling down on it she rushes off in search of a mattress. Next she decides that they need a pillow, and disappears again. Then she goes inside to look for a blanket. Finally she dashes off to fetch a bottle of perfumed oil. Kinesias is beginning to get cross:

> MYRRHINE: Here, take the bottle.
> KINESIAS: No thanks. I've got enough bottle down here. Lie down, damn you, don't bring any more things.
> MYRRHINE: I will, I swear it by Artemis. I'm just taking off my shoes. But look darling, don't forget about voting for peace.
> KINESIAS: I'll think about...
> (Myrrhine runs off into the Acropolis, and the doors are slammed behind her)
> She's gone. Hell's teeth, that woman. She set me on fire, got a good blaze going, put me through agonies, then just nipped off and left me.
>
> (ARISTOPHANES, *Lysistrata* 947-53)

Soon afterwards the Athenian men decide that they have had enough (or rather, not had enough), and make peace with the Spartans.

It is well known that in Classical Athens sexual love between men was accepted as perfectly normal; but this practice may not have affected relationships between husbands and wives to any great extent. For one thing, most of the evidence about male homosexuality relates to men from the upper classes, and it may not have been so common among those who were lower down the social scale. Secondly, the most common kind of affair seems to have been between a young man in his twenties and a youth whose beard had just begun to grow. Since most Athenian men married at about the age of thirty, the majority of homosexual relationships may have involved unmarried men. However, we do hear about a few older males who continued to see their boyfriends after they were married.

Sexual relationships between women are hardly ever mentioned by Athenian writers. Elsewhere they certainly existed. The poet Sappho, writing in the sixth century BC, speaks openly of her passionate attachment to other young women, with the result that in the nineteenth century the island where she lived, Lesbos, gave its name to female homosexuality. Respectable women in Sparta are also said to have had love affairs with unmarried girls. If lesbianism was practised in Athens, it seems strange that it receives no mention from Aristophanes, who is not normally noted for his reticence on sexual matters, especially where women are concerned. The explanation for this could be that it was fairly rare; alternatively, men may simply not have known about it, or indeed may have been so worried by it that it became a taboo subject.

'I would rather stand three times in the line of battle than give birth to a single child.'

These words, spoken by Medea in her long recital of women's wrongs (EURIPIDES, *Medea* 250-51), remind us of the dangers confronting Greek women when they went into labour. Most women would probably have had to face these dangers four or five times in their lifetime. Poor standards of hygiene and the very young age at which many women became pregnant would have contributed to the problems; and as many as one birth in five may have resulted in the death of the mother.

In normal circumstances childbirth seems to have been handled exclusively by women. Deliveries usually took place at home, and the mother would have had a midwife (a *maia*) and a network of female friends to help her. A doctor (almost always male) would have been summoned only in an emergency. At the moment of birth the women present shouted a triumphant *Ololuge*!, a ritual cry of joy. Then both the baby and its mother were given a bath to cleanse them from the ritual pollution of the birth process; and sometimes the infant was wrapped in swaddling-bands. The new arrival was announced to the community at large by pinning an appropriate symbol on the door of the house – an olive-crown for a boy, and a tuft of raw wool for a girl. In Italy today they use blue or pink ribbons in the same way. The *maia*'s duties probably included looking after the mother and child for several days after the birth.

One unpleasant task which also fell to the midwife was the organisation of the exposure of the baby, if for any reason it had been decided not to rear it. This would have involved taking the child to a rubbish dump or deserted spot and leaving it to die, unless it was picked up by a childless couple or someone wishing to rear a slave. Exposure may have been one of the methods used by the Athenians to control the size of their families, but it is very uncertain to what extent it was employed. All the references to it in Athenian literature are either general or mythological. The most famous example in myth is that of Oedipus, whose parents gave instructions for him to be abandoned on a mountain-side when he was a few days old, because an oracle had predicted that one day he would murder his father and marry his mother. The soft-hearted shepherd who was entrusted with the task took pity on him and gave him to another shepherd, who took him away to Corinth. When he was grown up Oedipus returned to Thebes, not realising that this was his birth-place, and there he fulfilled the oracle's predictions. He only discovered many years later the identity of a man he had murdered and of the woman he had subsequently married.

Although the circumstances would rarely have been so dramatic, exposure may have been viewed in real-life Classical Athens as an acceptable way of disposing of illegitimate, sickly or disabled babies. Whether healthy girl babies were also the regular victims of this kind of treatment, being considered less useful than boys, is difficult to say. The character who in a later comic play comments, 'Everybody raises a son, even if he is poor, but exposes a daughter even if he is rich', is probably exaggerating (POSIDIPPUS fragment 11, Kock). The disposal of girls may have been a measure resorted to from time to time by families who regarded them as an economic burden; however, it cannot have been practised on a widespread and systematic basis, as this would have resulted in a catastrophic population decline.

The decision to expose a legitimate child would have been taken by its father, and its mother may not have had much say in the matter. But a woman who gave birth to an illegitimate baby may have often been forced to carry out the deed herself. This agonising experience is movingly recalled by Creusa, a character in a play by Euripides who was the victim of a rape.

OLD SERVANT: Who exposed the child? Oh no, not you? surely not?
CREUSA: Yes. I did it. I swaddled him that night in my own dress.

OLD SERVANT: How could you bear to leave your own child inside that cave?
CREUSA: How? Yes, how? With many tearful goodbyes upon my lips, that was how I did it.
OLD SERVANT: So brave, so cruel...
CREUSA: Oh, you should have seen the baby stretching his hands towards me.
OLD SERVANT: Reaching for your breast, or to be cradled in your arms?
CREUSA: Yes. But he did not succeed

(EURIPIDES, *Ion* 954-63)

Offerings from grateful mothers (the contents of women's wardrobes)

At Brauron, the sanctuary where young Athenian women served Artemis before their marriages, the goddess also received offerings from women who had become wives and mothers. The inventories of treasures stored at the site include lists of splendid garments dedicated by women who were giving thanks to Artemis, as the goddess of childbirth, for their safe deliveries. These are some of the items mentioned, along with the names of their donors:

A little scalloped multi-coloured *chiton*, Kallipe; this has the letters woven into the pattern. Chairippe, Eukoline, a spotted garment in a wooden display box...Phile, a belt. Pheidylla, a white woman's *himation* in a display box. Mneso, a frog-green garment. Nausis, a lady's *himation* with a broad purple border in a wavy pattern around the edge. Kleo, a delicate shawl...Teisikrateia, a multi-coloured Persian style tunic with sleeves.

Contraception and abortion

Large families, with more than three or four children, seem to have been exceptional in ancient Athens. We have little knowledge of the methods used to limit family size, but certainly efficient contraception cannot have been among them. There is no evidence for the existence of anything resembling a condom in Classical Greece. All the contraceptive devices which we hear about are ones where the initiative lay with the woman; as usual, various pessaries, potions and ointments are recommended, and women also seem to have used tufts of fine raw wool to block the mouths of their wombs. None of these methods can possibly have worked very well, and the small size of Athenian families has to be accounted for by other factors. These may have included exposure, infant mortality, sexual abstinence, and abortion.

There was no blanket prohibition on abortion in Athens, either iegal or religious, although some kind of time limit may have been observed, and a married woman may in addition have been legally required to obtain the consent of her husband. Both Plato and Aristotle go so far as to recommend abortion as a means of controlling population growth. The clearest pronouncement against it is to be found in the Hippocratic oath, the vow taken by doctors, which was supposedly drawn up by the fifth-century physician Hippocrates. This includes the words, 'I will not give a pessary to cause abortion'. This declaration did not, however, prevent some of the medical writers from including prescriptions for abortive drugs in their treatises; while another author describes quite openly how he once advised a prostitute who was worried that she may have become pregnant to jump up and down seven times, touching her bottom with her heels, in order to expel 'the seed'. Many abortions seem to have been procured by women themselves, using pessaries and potions which they prepared at home. Surgical abortions, the most dangerous method, were apparently rare.

Murderous mothers

While grief-stricken mothers like Creusa, who mourn the loss of a child, make an occasional appearance in Athenian tragedy, they are not nearly so prominent as the mothers who are in conflict with their children, such as Clytemnestra. Sometimes a tragic mother goes even further, and murders her own son or sons. The most notable example is Euripides' heroine Medea, a desperately angry woman who has been deserted by her husband Jason. Though she dearly loves her sons, she steels herself to kill them because this is the most effective way she knows of winning revenge against Jason. Women in Athens were legally subordinate to men and had no official way of getting back at them when they were badly treated; but within the fictional families of Athenian tragedy they could wield tremendous power over their husbands by robbing them of their sons.

There is no evidence that in real life mothers abused or killed their children any more frequently than they do in our own society. Nevertheless, the female potential for domestic violence seems to have been a source of anxiety to Athenian men. This negative image of motherhood was also present in Greek myth. The ruling group of deities, known as the Olympians, included six goddesses. Of these, three were virgins, and had therefore renounced parenthood. The other three were sexually active and had produced offspring, but two of them, Aphrodite and Hera, were certainly not represented as loving mothers. Aphrodite had little or no contact with her children, while Hera on occasions was positively hostile to some of hers. Only Demeter, the goddess who went on strike in order to recover her daughter, presented an image of a selfless and devoted mother. So the ideal of motherhood which in our own society has been created by figures ranging from the Virgin Mary to the proud mum of the Persil adverts was largely absent from Greek culture. This gap is highlighted by the scarcity of mother and child groups in the visual arts. In vase-paintings women in the home are far more likely to be working wool, an activity which we shall be looking at in a later section, than caring for children.

It is not particularly easy to understand Athenian men's reservations about motherhood, especially when so much stress was placed on the child-bearing role. Perhaps many of them had had difficult relationships with their mothers. Up to the age of six young boys would have spent most of their time in the female environment of the home with their mothers, sisters and female slaves. After this they were introduced to the outside world of school, gymnasium, army, and political institutions, and were initiated into a masculine culture which to a very great extent excluded women. Hence close contact with their mothers would have been followed by a lifestyle in which women were viewed as belonging almost to a different species, and this process could well have produced emotional tensions between mothers and sons.

In addition the role which Athenian society had assigned to women could have created a kind of collective anxiety about mothers. Their task of providing legitimate heirs was seen as vital, and there would have been a great deal of concern that they might not do this job properly. The fact that women, though desperately needed, had also been excluded from any form of economic or political power would only have increased these worries. The heroine Medea, who makes a passionate speech about the wrongs of women and later murders her sons, illustrates very well the fears which the male imagination must have harboured concerning frustrated females, and the power they possessed as mothers.

Xenokleia, a heart-broken mother

As far as we know, these fears were largely unfounded: mothers in real life seem to have been just as caring as they are today. The devotion of one of them, who lived in Athens' port of Piraeus in the fourth century BC, is recorded in her epitaph:

> Leaving two young daughters, Xenokleia, daughter of Nikarchos, lies here dead; she mourned the sorrowful end of her son, Phoenix, who died out at sea when he was eight years old. There is no-one who is so unacquainted with mourning, Xenokleia, that he does not feel pity for your fate. You left behind two young girls and died of yearning for your son, who has a pitiless tomb where he lies in the dark sea.

Divorce

In legal terms divorce was easy in Athens, since there was no need to go to court. The great majority of divorces were initiated by the husband, who simply had to send his wife back home to live with her family. Failure to produce children was probably the most common cause, and the man's aim would have been to acquire another wife who would hopefully give birth to sons. Falling in love with another woman would rarely have been a factor, since as we have seen romantic love was not generally regarded as a basis for marriage. The children of a divorced couple seem in most cases to have remained with the father.

Although it was perfectly possible, it was unusual for a divorce to be initiated by the wife or her family. When this did happen, the woman's male next-of-kin acted on her behalf, and removed her from her husband's home; he probably had the right to do this even without the woman's consent. Occasionally the prospect of a more profitable match would have been the motive. In one comedy by an anonymous author of the fourth or third century BC (attributed at one time to the playwright Menander), a distraught daughter begs her father not to marry her off to a richer husband:

> If my husband has done me some harm, I am the one who ought to have noticed it. But I am quite unaware of it. Perhaps I am stupid. But, father, even if a woman is a foolish creature when it comes to other matters, about her own affairs perhaps she has some sense. Well, let us assume you are right. Explain to me then in what way he has done me wrong. There is a covenant between husband and wife; he must cherish her always, until the end, and she must do her best to please her husband in all things. He has been everything to me that I could have wanted,

and what pleases him pleases me also, father. So, he is a good husband as far as I am concerned; but he has fallen on hard times, and you, so you say, now want to marry me to a rich man so that I shall not live out my life in distress. Where does so much money exist, father, that having it can make me happier than my husband does? How can it be just or right that I should take a share in the good things he has, but take no share in his poverty? Tell me, if the man who is intending to marry me – dear God, may it never happen, nor will it happen if I have anything to do with it – if this man too loses his livelihood, will you marry me off to another husband? And if that one grows poor, to yet another? How long will you go on cheating fortune with regards to my life, father?.... So do not, in the name of Hestia, rob me of the husband to whom you gave me. The favour I am asking is just and humane, father.

(*Menander*, edited Sandbach, p.328, 8-40).

The other woman. Mistresses and adultery

The 'everyday needs of the body', according to one law-court speaker, were satisfied by mistresses. This term was used to describe any woman who was living with a man on a more or less permanent basis and was not formally married to him. Presumably most men could not have afforded to keep a mistress as well as a wife; but the practice seems to have been relatively common among upper-class males. Although the majority of mistresses were slaves or foreigners, a few were free-born Athenians, presumably women whose families were too poor to afford dowries. They received some protection under Athenian law, since they came under their partners' guardianship, and could therefore expect to be maintained by them. While separate establishments seem to have been the normal rule, occasionally a wife may have had to share her home with her husband's mistress.

In Athenian terms these extra-marital relationships did not constitute adultery. The Greek word *moicheia*, normally translated as adultery, actually has a rather different meaning, and the phrase 'illicit sex' would probably represent it more accurately. In Athens it was illegal for a man to have sexual intercourse with an Athenian woman who came under the guardianship of another Athenian citizen, and who was not registered as a prostitute. This meant that among local women men were legally restricted to sexual relations with their wives or mistresses. But non-Athenian women were another matter. There was no legal or apparently moral bar on relations with prostitutes, slaves, or resident aliens. These affairs did not, in the male-dominated Athenian value-system, count as *moicheia*. Indeed, the marital status of the man involved in a relationship was entirely irrelevant. The social status of the woman – whether or not she was Athenian, and whether or not she 'belonged' to another man – was all that mattered. The main purpose seems to have been to guarantee the paternity of sons who would one day receive the benefits of inheritance and of Athenian citizenship. As far as women were concerned this meant that during the whole of their lives they were restricted by law to sexual relations with their husbands. In other words, double standards were operating.

Any citizen who caught a man in the act of having sex with a woman who was under his guardianship had the right to kill him on the spot. Drastic self-help remedies of this kind were rare, however, for the man ran the risk of being prosecuted for homicide, and would need to prove in court that he had actually found the couple in bed together. Various alternative courses of action were available. The aggrieved husband or father could accept financial compensation from the seducer, or could subject him to various bodily humiliations, including, it seems, what Aristophanes refers to as 'radishment' – having a large radish stuffed up his anus. If he preferred to hand over the task of punishing the offender to the state, he could bring a prosecution for *moicheia*. This offence covered rape as well as seduction, and in both cases the maximum penalty was death, although a fine might be imposed as an alternative.

The punishments inflicted on the erring woman seem to us to be less severe, but they might nevertheless have a devastating effect on her life. Her husband was legally obliged to divorce her, and she was barred from all public religious celebrations. Any man who met her at a religious event had the right to tear her clothes off and beat her, though he must stop short of killing her. Since religion was an enormously important part of the social life of Athenian women, a ban of this sort would have amounted to public disgrace.

Aristotle's mistress

In his will the philosopher made careful provision for Herpyllis, the woman who had been his mistress:

> The executors and Nikanor, in memory of me and of the steady affection which Herpyllis always showed me, shall take care of her in every way, and if she wishes to be married shall see to it

that she is given to one who is not unworthy.

(DIOGENES LAERTIUS 5.13)

Under the terms of the will Herpyllis was to receive a talent of silver, three slave-girls, a man-servant, a house and some furniture, which she was to choose herself. But Aristotle also requested that he should be buried alongside the bones of his wife.

The wife of Euphiletos

We do know of one case where a husband took advantage of his right to take the law into his own hands, and killed the man whom he allegedly found in his wife's bed. The murdered man's family certainly contested this last claim, because later they prosecuted the husband for homicide, presumably denying that their relative, Eratosthenes, had ever been the woman's lover. The prosecution speech does not survive, but the one which the husband Euphiletos made in his own defence, composed for him by the speech-writer Lysias, has been preserved. What follows is a summary of this tale of seduction and adultery. Unhappily the name of its star, the speaker's allegedly unfaithful wife, is unknown to us. Masculine concern about protecting an Athenian woman's modesty extended to a ban on speaking her name in public, even when she was being accused of behaviour which was rather less than modest. Instead, women were referred to as some man's wife, mother, sister or daughter.

Euphiletos is careful to state that the affair between Eratosthenes and his wife only began after the birth of their son. When they were first married Euphiletos had carefully supervised his wife's activities, but once the child had been born he began to place more trust in her. The young man Eratosthenes actually saw his wife for the first time at the funeral of Euphiletos' own mother, though he did not speak to her on that occasion. A funeral would probably not have been an ideal venue for conducting a flirtation; however, family rituals of this kind did provide women with a rare opportunity for seeing men who were not close relatives, so it would not be altogether surprising if the couple made meaningful eye contact on that occasion. Soon afterwards Eratosthenes met Euphiletos' maid on her way to the market, and got in touch with the wife by using this girl as a go-between. Eventually he began coming to the house while the husband was away on the family farm.

Euphiletos' house had two storeys, and when he was first married the women's quarters were on the upper floor. After the birth of the baby this arrangement was changed, and the women moved to the ground floor so that the wife could wash the child more easily (the well was presumably in the courtyard of the house). The couple's bedroom was on the upper floor, although his wife often slept downstairs because she used to feed the baby during the night. One evening when Euphiletos came back unexpectedly from the country the pair retired to bed together, but in the night the baby started crying, and Euphiletos insisted that his wife go down to feed it. She started to tease him, claiming that he only wanted her to go downstairs so that he could get his hands on the pretty slave-girl; and then she playfully turned the key in the bedroom lock when she left, returning only at dawn. Later Euphiletos realised that the lover must have been in the house, and that the slave had been making the baby cry on purpose. He did notice the next day that his wife was wearing make-up, even though she was still in mourning for one of her brothers. But he thought no more about it.

A few days later Euphiletos was stopped in the street by an old woman sent to waylay him by one of Eratosthenes' jealous mistresses. She gave him a brief account of the affair with his wife and of the young man's other escapades. He went home at once and extracted more of the details from the maid, after threatening her with a whipping. The next time Eratosthenes entered the house, after Euphiletos had gone to bed, the maid went to wake her master:

> I told her to watch the door, and left the house very quietly. I
> called on one friend after another,...took with me as many of
> them as I could, and went back home.... We pushed open the
> door of the bedroom, and the first of us to enter the room were
> in time to see him lying down beside my wife. Those who were
> behind saw him standing naked on the bed. I hit him and
> knocked him down, then tied his hands behind his back.
> (LYSIAS 1.23-4)

According to Euphiletos, Eratosthenes admitted his guilt, and begged his captor not to kill him. His pleas were in vain.

Sadly, we do not know the outcome of this gripping case. Many modern readers find it difficult to sympathise with Euphiletos, who seems a stuffy and self-righteous character, while his wife emerges from the story as a lively and enterprising woman. Given the gloomy view of women's restricted lives often presented by Greek writers, it is rather refreshing to learn that, in spite of being largely confined to the home, this wife still had enough freedom to conduct a passionate affair almost under her husband's nose.

We have almost no idea how frequent love affairs of this kind were. Some of the female characters in Aristophanes' comedies refer to their lovers as though they were a standard accessory. In one play, for example, the heroine Praxagora is extolling the traditional values of women, and exclaims:

> They bake muffins, as they've always done.
> They nag their husbands, as they've always done.
> They hide their lovers in the house, as they've always done.
> They buy goodies on the sly, as they've always done.
> They love neat wine, as they've always done.
> They enjoy a bit of bonking on the side, as they've always done.
>
> (ARISTOPHANES, *Women in the Assembly* 223-8)

This is an old joke about women. As we have seen, it belongs to a culture in which exaggerated claims about the female sexual appetite (and their appetite for alcohol) helped to justify the maintenance of masculine control over women's bodies. It seems unlikely that adultery was very common among the women of Athens, simply because they had so few opportunities for meeting potential lovers. But most Athenian men would have had little idea what their wives got up to when they were away from home. Male writers who refer in glowing terms to the purity of their womenfolk are not necessarily any more reliable as informants than a comic playwright who specialises in sexual innuendo.

The women's rooms

The 'women's quarters' (*gynaikonitis*) mentioned by Euphiletos in the previous section would probably have been a feature of most Greek houses; but they were not necessarily given a permanent location, or situated in the remotest part of the house. In the ancient Greek home rooms were versatile, and their functions would have changed as domestic situations altered. The women's quarters were simply the room or rooms where the female members of the household worked and slept, with any space that was left over being used by the menfolk and their visitors. In most houses the living accommodation was arranged around an internal courtyard, and in spring and summer the women would often have worked, relaxed and eaten their meals in this outdoor area. So in many cases the women's quarters would have consisted in practice of the courtyard and a couple of adjacent rooms.

The domestic duties of a wife

An invented model husband called Ischomachos is used in a treatise by Xenophon as the mouthpiece for a detailed set of pronouncements on the management of the *oikos*, or household. One of the foremost responsibilities of a competent head of household, according to Ischomachos, is the careful training of one's wife. His own spouse, he tells us, was only fifteen years old when he married her. She had been brought up knowing nothing of the world, but in her parents' home she had at least been taught how to spin and weave wool, and how to allocate this kind work to female slaves.

Ischomachos only began his own course of instruction after he had made sure that his wife was 'sufficiently pliable and domesticated to carry on a conversation' (XENOPHON, *Household management* 7.10). Then he explained to her, very kindly, that their roles in maintaining an orderly household would be complementary. Human beings, he told her, need shelter for the storage of goods, for the rearing of children and for the production of food and clothing. While men are constitutionally suited to hard outdoor work, women – being naturally more soft, tender and anxious than men – are better qualified for the indoor tasks:

> 'So it is fitting that a woman should remain inside and not venture out of doors; but for a man to stay indoors and not attend to the work outside the house is disgraceful.' (7.30)

A woman, Ischomachos said, is like a queen bee. She despatches others to their jobs outside the home, supervises those who work inside, and stores, administers and distributes the goods that are brought into the house from the farm:

> 'Take care that the goods laid by for a year aren't used up in a month. And when the wool is brought to you, you must make sure that cloaks are made for those that need them. You must also see to it that the dry corn is in a good condition for making food.' (7.36)

In addition she must take care of the slaves when they fall sick, train the new ones, and discipline and punish those that are negligent or dishonest.

Afterwards Ischomachos gave his bride a practical lesson on the organisation of domestic space:

'There is nothing, oh wife, so convenient or good for human beings as order.... What a beautiful sight it is when boots of all sorts and conditions are arranged in rows, when cloaks of all sorts are kept separate, or blankets, or cooking pots, or side-tables... there is beauty even in an arrangement of casserole dishes when they are neatly displayed.'   (8.3,19)

He took her on a tour of the house, pointing out the best locations for store-rooms, living-rooms, and the women's quarters. The last were to be 'divided from the men's apartments by a bolted door, so that the slaves could not breed without their owners' permission' (9.5). Only slaves who were well behaved were to be allowed to take partners and produce children. Then he moved on to the storage arrangements and drew up an enormously detailed master plan for the distribution of household items. In Ischomachos' *oikos* everything was to have its own special place, matching the separate spheres which, according to him, nature had assigned to men and women in the wider world.

The poor woman's training was still not complete. One day Ischomachos noticed that she was wearing make-up and high heels; he reprimanded her gently, delivering a short lecture on the value of natural beauty. When he asked her how she would feel if he were the one using blusher and foundation, she cried, 'I would much rather touch the real you than a smear of red paint!'. How silly she was then to believe that she could practise this kind of deception on him, for he was able to see her in the morning, before she applied her make-up, not to mention those occasions when she was crying or sweating or washing her face. If she wanted to keep her good looks, he said, she should avoid too much sitting about. Instead she should stand over the slaves and supervise them while they were doing the housework, and when she was in need of more vigorous exercise she could knead and roll out dough, shake out cloaks, and make the bed. Conveniently enough, domestic duties provided a woman with her most effective beauty treatment.

To most modern readers Ischomachos seems terribly fussy and patronising; but some of them will probably agree with him when he maintains that females and males are genetically equipped with separate characteristics, and that these complement each other in the partnership of marriage. We must also give him credit for the great respect which he shows for his wife's managerial role within the home, while bearing in mind that this respect may not have been shared by many real-life Athenian husbands. However, in spite of the responsibilities placed on the woman of the family, the treatise makes it perfectly clear who is in charge in this particular household: if Ischomachos' bride represents the Athenian notion of an ideal wife, then we have to admit that she was a docile and obedient creature. The fictional Ischomachos was clearly a wealthy man, and most households would not have possessed as many slaves as his did. Euphiletos' 'middle-income' family is probably more typical, with a single slave-girl employed as a domestic servant. The woman who lived in a household like this would have found that she had plenty of work to do to keep her inside the home, even though in theory she may have been free to go out of doors. 'It's difficult for a woman to get out of the house. What with dancing attendance on her husband, keeping the slave-girl on her toes, putting the baby to bed, bathing it, feeding it', is the comment made by one of the female agitators in Aristophanes' *Lysistrata* (16-19). In poorer households with no slaves women would have had to do all the cooking, cleaning, spinning, weaving, and washing as well; and those who lived in the country would also have helped on the farm.

A power-base in the home?

It is impossible to know how many Athenian wives 'lived up' to the masculine ideal of submissiveness represented by Ischomachos' bride. Although women were totally excluded from the political arena, within the home some of them may have exercised more authority. As we have seen, Athenian tragedies like *Medea* pictured women who by devious and often violent means managed to gain power over their husbands. More realistic are the women in Aristophanes' comedies, who get their own way by nagging, by doing things behind their husbands' backs or by refusing to have sex with them. Sometimes women handled all the family finances: in *Lysistrata*, when an Athenian magistrate protests at the idea of women taking over the state treasury, the heroine retorts, 'What's so peculiar about that? We've been in charge of the housekeeping for years, haven't we?' (ARISTOPHANES, *Lysistrata* 494-5). There may have been many Athenian husbands who, like the fictional Ischomachos, spent most of their time out of doors, and allowed their wives a fair degree of freedom in the day-to-day running of the household. This would help to explain why there was so much male anxiety about what women were getting up to at home. But it is also clear that in theory at least, and probably often in practice, the ultimate responsibility for the *oikos* lay with its male *kyrios*. Although there may have been a certain amount of hidden female power to be discovered behind the closed doors of Athenian dwellings, in most cases it would have been strictly limited.

A mother who can read account books

Some women may have become more assertive when their children's interests were under threat. In one law-court speech we hear about a widow whose two sons were thrown out of their guardian's house when the elder boy came of age, and were given only a meagre portion of their inheritance. Their mother implored one of her relatives to arrange a meeting with the guardian and the other members of the family, 'saying that even though she had no previous experience of speaking in the presence of men, the severity of their misfortunes would force her to give us a full account of their troubles.' (LYSIAS 32.11). At the meeting this determined woman produced some account books which her sons had found in the house. With these she was able to prove that the unscrupulous guardian, who was her own father, had received large sums of money from her deceased husband's estate:

'You are wronging my children...and feel neither fear of the gods nor shame before me, though I am in full possession of all the facts.'   (LYSIAS 32.17)

Here at least was was one Athenian woman who was not afraid to speak her mind in male company; and who was also capable of reading and understanding financial accounts.

Xanthippe, a nagging wife and mother

It cannot have been a great deal of fun being married to the philosopher Socrates. Not only was he infuriatingly addicted to hair-splitting arguments, but what with his political duties, his work as a sculptor, and his interminable dialogues with his pupils, he must have spent even less time at home than other Athenian men. So it is little wonder that Xanthippe, his long suffering spouse, earned a reputation as a whingeing wife. When a fellow guest at a symposium asked Socrates why a man of his wisdom did not set about training his wife, who in his opinion was the most bad-tempered woman the world had ever seen, the philosopher replied:

'Because...it is my ambition to tackle and associate with mankind as a whole; and I am well aware that if I can put up with her, I shall have no trouble at all in my dealings with the rest of the human race.'   (XENOPHON, *Symposium* 2.10)

Poor Xanthippe seems to have had an even more difficult time with her son Lamprokles. On one occasion Socrates was telling him off for being so rude to his mother; he went on and on about all the pain and toil which mothers endure for the sake of their sons:

> LAMPROKLES: But even if she has done all of these things and far more, no-one could possibly put up with her vile temper.
> SOCRATES: Which is harder to bear, a wild animal's ferocity, or a mother's?
> LAMPROKLES: I'd say a mother's, if she's anything like mine.
> (XENOPHON, *Memorabilia* 2.2.7)

When Socrates was about to be executed for impiety, Xanthippe visited him in prison. She broke into loud wails when some of his friends arrived, and cried, 'Oh, Socrates, this is the last time you and your friends will talk together'. 'Someone had better take her home,' Socrates said (PLATO, *Phaedo* 60a).

A wicked wife and stepmother?

Wives were occasionally a lot more troublesome than poor Xanthippe, or so it is claimed. A man named Philoneos once invited a friend of his to dine with him at his house in Piraeus, the port of Athens; his mistress, who was a slave, served them with wine after the meal. Both were taken ill, and Philoneos died at once – his friend lingered on for another three weeks before finally succumbing to the poison. The mistress was tortured and put to death.

Some time later the illegitimate son of the friend charged his father's wife, who was his stepmother, with murdering both his father and Philoneos. The mistress, he maintained, was only an accessory. His stepmother had made friends with her deliberately, knowing that she was about to be deserted by Philoneos, and had pretended to be in a similar position herself. A love-philtre dropped into the wine would revive their partners' affections, she said, so she handed over a potion which was in reality a poison:

> The subordinate who carried out the deed has been punished as she deserved, although she was not the instigator of the crime.... The woman who instigated and planned it will also suffer a just penalty, members of the jury, if you and the gods so will it. (ANTIPHON, *Prosecution of a stepmother* 27)

We have no knowledge of the outcome of this case, or the truth of the stepson's allegations. But it is hard to believe that the mistress, when tortured, would not have revealed the name of the woman who had got her into this appalling situation.

Cosmetics and accessories

The make-up which Ischomachos' wife was caught wearing consisted of a liquid foundation, made from white lead, and a blusher. In a fragment from one lost comedy we hear some masculine jokes about the vast array of beauty aids used by women:

> Here's a razor, a mirror, some scissors, a lip-salve,
> A hair-piece, slides, ribbons, some hairbands,
> Blusher, some 'feminine products', a foundation,
> Perfume, an emery-board, bras, some false curls,
> A veil, rouge, two necklaces, eye-shadow,
> A see-through nightie, a well-trimmed bush, a hair-net,
> A girdle, a silk body...
> (ARISTOPHANES, fragment 320K, Edmunds, p. 663)

The wool-working woman

Ischomachos' young bride may have been brought up in girlish ignorance, but she did at least know how to work wool. The manufacture of textiles was seen by Greek men as the archetypal feminine accomplishment. It was used, for example, by the Trojan hero Hector in Homer's *Iliad* to mark the distinction between male and female spheres of activity. When his wife Andromache tries to persuade him not to return to the battlefield, he tells her, 'Go back to the house then, and attend to your own work, the loom and the distaff, and see to it that your handmaidens ply their work also; but let the men take care of the war...' (*Iliad* 6.490-2).

In Classical Athens the majority of textiles were still manufactured by women working in the home. Wool was by far the most common fabric, though linen, valued for its softness, was sometimes produced in the wealthier households; cotton was as yet unknown in Greece. Wool-making was laborious and time-consuming work, involving a number of processes – detaching the wool from the fleeces, cleaning, untangling and combing it, dyeing and spinning it, and finally weaving it into cloth on a loom (Figs. 16 and 17, pp. 42, 66). It may have taken as long as six weeks for one woman to produce enough material to make up a *peplos* or *chiton*. In better-off families, of course, female slaves would have done most of the work, but the wife would have had a supervisory role and would also have helped with the spinning and weaving. Through

Fig. 17 A painting showing various stages in the manufacture of textiles. The arms on the far left belong to a woman who is spinning, while the woman next to her is drawing raw wool from a basket so that it can be spun. The two women to the right of her are weaving at a loom, a job that was done in a standing position. A black-figure *lekythos*, or oil-jar, c.540 BC.

work like this women would have supplied all the clothing needed in the household, and most of its soft furnishings, including wall-hangings, cushions and bedcovers. Weaving in particular required great skill, and women clearly took tremendous pride in the intricacy and inventiveness of their designs.

Men too seem to have had a high regard for the art of wool-working. It is far and away the most common of all the indoor tasks which we see women performing in vase-paintings; and it is even represented on the pots in which wine was served at all-male drinking parties, or *symposia*. We can easily imagine that to a male viewer the image of a wool-working woman would in most contexts have signified a virtuous wife, devoted to the well-being of her family and fully occupied at home, with no time for gossip or gadding about. The textiles which were the products of these women's labours were also highly valued. Examples of their handiwork, in the form of cushions and couch-covers, would have been displayed in the most public part of the house, the men's dining-room in which *symposia* were held. Here they would have served to advertise the virtues and skills of the female members of the household.

Spinning and weaving were services which women performed not just for their families, but also for deities. Statues of gods and goddesses were sometimes adorned with clothing, and the offerings displayed in sanctuaries often included garments dedicated by women worshippers. As we have seen, various items of clothing were presented to Artemis, in her sanctuary at Brauron, by mothers who had survived the rigours of childbirth. In Athens, the most prestigious textile received by a deity was certainly the *peplos* which was presented to the statue of Athena Polias at the culmination of the Great Panathenaia festival (Fig. 6, p. 12). A new one was woven for every festival by a team of specially chosen young women; but the same scene was always depicted, the battle between the Gods and the Giants.

A woman with her hands full

Spinning was the most time-consuming of all the wool-working processes. Women in the country would probably have gone out of doors with their distaffs and spindles, and done other jobs at the same time. The Persian king Darius was once enormously impressed by the number of tasks he saw one woman performing simultaneously:

> The girl, on reaching the river, watered the horse, filled her pitcher, and started walking back with the pitcher of water on her head, leading the horse with one hand, and turning her spindle.

> (HERODOTUS 5.12)

Working from home: Aristarchos' relatives

One day Socrates bumped into a friend of his, a man called Aristarchos, who was looking awfully worried. He explained that during the turmoil caused by a recent political coup a number of his sisters, cousins and nieces had been made homeless. A group of them had moved *en masse* into his house, with the result that he now had to support no fewer than fourteen people. 'It's hard to see one's family die', he said, 'but I can't feed that number in times like this'.

After some argument Socrates managed to convince Aristarchos that if slaves could earn their own living, so could free women. There was nothing disgraceful in honest work, and what could be more useful than making clothes, a job that women thoroughly understood? Eventually Aristarchos decided to borrow a bit of capital and invest it in raw wool:

> As a result the women used to work through their lunch-hour, only stopping at supper-time; and there were happy instead of gloomy faces....They loved Aristarchos as their saviour, and he was fond of them because they were useful. Finally Aristarchos came to see Socrates, and explained all this to him delightedly. 'Their only complaint,' he said, 'is that I am the only person in the house who isn't earning his own livelihood.'
>
> (XENOPHON, *Memorabilia* 2.7.12)

The unravelling of domestic order

If the presence of a wool-working woman in the home meant that all was well with the world, then a woman who had abandoned her loom signified the opposite. In Euripides' *Bacchae*, when women worshippers rush out of the city to dance for the god Dionysos on the mountain-side, men feel that the world has been turned upside down and civilisation is collapsing:

> ...In the mountains they linger,
> That throng of wild women,
> Driven away from their shuttles and looms
> By the frenzy of Dionysos.
>
> (EURIPIDES, *Bacchae* 116-19)

Weaving wisdom, weaving wiles

So wool-working could be used to signify both the proper performance of domestic duties and the breakdown of domestic order. Indeed, it was so closely identified with women that it could serve as a symbol of many aspects of their activities. In particular it was associated with female knowledge, and hence with a kind of female power. Knowledge arises from the use of language, and language and woven cloth are often linked together in Greek thought. There were probably two reasons for this. Firstly, the processes were seen as similar – syllables could be joined together to make words, and words combined into narratives, just as threads were interlaced to produce cloth. In the same way we still speak today of 'weaving tales'. Secondly, women could weave figure-scenes into their textiles, and so could use them quite literally to tell stories. For example, when we first meet Helen in the *Iliad* she is weaving the story of the Trojan War which is being fought outside on the battlefield *(Iliad* 3.121-8). In later times tapestries like the one at Bayeux were used in a similar manner to record recent events.

However, material did not have to tell stories in order to convey knowledge to women. Weaving was a kind of hand-writing, and women were perfectly capable of recognising cloth which they had made themselves, just as women today can often recognise their own knitting. Sometimes in tragedies this helps them to learn the truth about another person's identity. In Aeschylus' *Libation-bearers* (231-2) Elektra is reunited with her long-lost brother Orestes when he produces a piece of material which she wove as a girl; while Creusa in Euripides' *Ion* (1417-25) is able to identify her grown-up son through a coverlet which she tucked into his cradle when she abandoned him as a baby.

Material can also be used to cover and conceal, so that weaving is associated with women's deceptions as well as their knowledge. The most celebrated of all Greek wool-workers, Penelope, declares in the *Odyssey*, 'I weave my own wiles'. During her husband's lengthy absence she resisted the pressure to remarry by telling her numerous suitors that they would have to wait until she had finished making a shroud for her father- in-law. For three years, during daylight hours, she sat at her loom weaving. At night-time she had torches lit, and unravelled what she had woven during the day. Eventually one of her maidservants spilt the beans to the suitors and she was forced to finish her work *(Odyssey* 19.137-161). By employing this famous trick Penelope managed, temporarily, to gain control of a difficult situation. Wool-working, then, was seen as something which could make a woman powerful. On the level of the divine it was used to symbolise the authority exercised by figures like the Fates, who spin a man's destiny 'with the thread at his birth' (*Odyssey* 7.198), or by the goddess Athena, who was patron deity of spinning and weaving.

As a means of communication and a source of power exclusive to women, wool-working could also be seen as dangerous to men. It seems to have been used to express the kind of fears about women which we looked at in relation to murderous mothers. This is best illustrated by the myth of the Thracian ruler Tereus, who raped his sister-in-law Philomela and then tried to silence her by cutting out her tongue. Philomela outwitted him by weaving the story of this assault into a tapestry and sending it to her sister Prokne. The two women went on to win a terrible revenge. They butchered Itys, the son of Tereus and Prokne, and then tricked the king into eating him when he was served up in a stew. Other stories stress the lethal quality of garments themselves. The hero Heracles dies a horrible death when he is presented by his wife Deianeira with a tunic which she has doused in poison, believing it to be a love-potion (SOPHOCLES, *Women of Trachis* 749-812). Another hero, Jason, is brought to ruin when his jilted wife Medea murders his new bride with a beautiful poisoned dress (EURIPIDES, *Medea* 1136-1203), and then goes on to slaughter their sons. The effects of this terrible garment are later described by a messenger:

> Her flesh, gnawed by the unseen fangs of the poison,
> Dripped from her bones like gum from a fir-tree,
> A terrible sight. No-one dared touch her body.
>
> (EURIPIDES, *Medea* 1200-03)

The power which these fictional women exert through their wool-working is sometimes equated with their sexual power. In the *Odyssey*, for example, some of the sexiest female characters are women who spin or weave. Notable among these is the enchantress Circe, who when visited by Odysseus' men was 'singing in a sweet voice/as she went up and down a great design on a loom'. She invited Odysseus into her bed, but he knew that once he was naked she would make him 'weak and unmanly' unless he bound her by a solemn oath not to do him any harm (*Odyssey* 10.221-2, 341).

In Athenian vase-painting textile production and sex are most strikingly combined in the figures known as 'the spinning prostitutes', women who are shown in the middle of brothel scenes calmly spinning wool. It is not at all easy to explain these images, although we do need to bear in mind that in real life prostitutes may well have whiled away their spare mornings making fabric. The viewer may also have been aware of wool-making's symbolic links with sex: distaffs and spindles may have been seen as phallic objects. Weaving was certainly regarded as a parallel process to sexual intercourse, since it involved the interlacing of stiff vertical

Fig. 18 A woman holding a flower, with a *kalathos* or wool-basket on the floor behind her. There is a mirror hanging on the wall above the basket, and to the left there is the edge of a couch. The interior of a red-figure cup, c.480 BC.

threads (the 'masculine' warp) and softer horizontal threads (the 'feminine' weft). Moreover, as a creative activity which was exclusive to women it could be thought of as resembling their main creative function, that of producing babies (Fig. 16, p. 42). The same association of ideas was probably present in the various references to wool-working at weddings. Gifts to the bride, for example, generally included a *kalathos*, or wool-basket. The jar in Fig. 17 (p. 66) showing the various stages of wool-working was probably a woman's wedding present.

Wool-working, then, was an activity which could be used to denote a dutiful wife and mother; but such was the ambiguity of the male response to women, and to their sexuality, that in certain contexts it could conjure up a set of rather more disturbing ideas. It could allude to women's knowledge, to their deceitfulness, to their capacity for taking control of events, to their murderous tendencies, and to a sexual power which threatened to overwhelm men if not handled carefully. One interesting effect of this range of allusions is that as a symbol wool-working itself was often ambiguous. In Fig. 18, which shows the inside of a wine-cup, a woman is seen with various items which refer to her beauty and her sexual identity – a flower, a mirror, and the edge of a couch. The object standing at her feet is a *kalathos*, used for holding raw or spun wool. Although the scene on the outside of the cup depicts young men negotiating with streetwalkers, we have no way of knowing whether the woman who appears on the inside is a good wife or a prostitute. The wool-basket in itself does not help us to distinguish between these two types of female.

Indoors and outdoors

Athenian women, as we have seen, were associated with hidden interiors in a number of ways. Unlike men, they were nearly always shown in sculpture and painting safely wrapped up in their clothes. They themselves were thought of as containing interior spaces which needed to be filled by men and by babies. Finally, the stress on female chastity meant that women were supposed to remain indoors as much as possible, a rule which was reinforced by the theory that they had been shaped by nature for the performance of domestic tasks.

Male citizens, on the other hand, were associated with the outdoor world. Most of them worked outside the home, on farms or in workshops, and also took part in collective leisure activities such as athletics. In addition, many of them served in the army or navy, and were actively involved in democratic politics. As the statesman Pericles said in his famous funeral speech, 'We regard the man who plays no part in public affairs, not as one who minds his own business, but as a person who is good for nothing' (THUCYDIDES 2.40.2). So in Athens the gap between masculine and feminine spheres of activity seemed particularly wide, and was often expressed as a contrast between public and private domains. The hidden quality of women's lives, their 'underground and shadowy existence' (PLATO, *Laws* 781c), would have contributed to men's belief that females were secretive and possibly even dangerous.

But were women in Athens really confined to the domestic interior? There can be no doubt that among the upper classes it was seen as a mark of wealth, status and respectability if a man was able to avoid the need for his womenfolk to go out of doors. The seclusion of women within the home had developed into an ideal, which other social classes tried, with varying degrees of success, to follow. When Ischomachos' wife used make-up on her face she was attempting to make it look paler, a fashion created by this notion that genteel women spent all their time indoors and, unlike men, never became tanned. Some years ago our own society experienced the opposite trend, when the ideal of a healthy outdoor life, coupled with the popularity of foreign holidays, produced a fashion for sun-tans.

Even within the home women were supposed to be kept apart from males who were not their relatives. A woman who answered the front door herself was considered in some circles to be almost a slut; while a man who entered another citizen's house without being invited, and ran across his wife and daughters, had in most people's view committed a monstrous act. If male guests were present the women of the house ate apart from the men; and the only females who attended the *symposium* were entertainers or prostitutes.

It was probably only among the relatively well-off that the ideal of female seclusion could be put into practice effectively. For, as Aristotle said, in a democratic society 'who could prevent the wives of the poor from going out when they want to?' (ARISTOTLE, *Politics* 1300a). In houses where there was no well in the courtyard and no slave-girl to fetch water women would have made regular trips to the public fountain (Fig. 19, p. 74). Female friendships, though not discussed a great deal by male writers, certainly existed; and we know that women visited each other in their homes to borrow salt, help a woman in labour, or celebrate the birth of a baby. Even upper-class women would have been expected to appear in public when they were performing religious duties or attending weddings or funerals.

In addition, poorer women would sometimes have had to leave their homes in order to go to work. 'We do not live in the way we would like' is the bitter comment of one law-court speaker whose family had fallen on hard times (DEMOSTHENES, 57.31). During the difficult years following Athens' defeat in the Peloponnesian War his mother had been forced to earn her living as a nurse and a ribbon-seller. Other women of the citizen class found work as midwives, washerwomen and casual agricultural labourers. In many of these jobs the women would not have been required to speak to men, so a kind of segregation could still be observed.

But this was not always the case. Though citizen women do not seem to have done the shopping (this was a task for slaves or for the man of the house), this did not prevent some of them from running stalls in the market-place selling flowers, vegetables or bread. In these circumstances the pretence that in the public arena women were both silent and invisible would have been hard to maintain.

Fig. 19 Women drawing water at a public fountain. Black-figure *hydria*, or water-jar, c.520 BC.

An easing of the pressure on women to remain at home would probably have occurred in the course of the Peloponnesian War. At the beginning of the conflict the Athenians had been obliged to evacuate the country-side and bring the rural population inside the city walls to protect them from attack by the Spartans. This caused terrible overcrowding in the city, and in many households seclusion would have been hard to maintain at such times. Countrywomen, in addition, would have been used to popping outdoors to feed the chickens or milk the goat, and may not have been prepared to change their ways when they moved into the urban centre. Women in general probably felt more free when so many men were absent at the war, and as we know some of them had been forced by growing financial hardship to look for work outside the home. At the same time the disasters suffered in the war meant that Athenian men were becoming increasingly disillusioned with public life, and were setting a higher value on private fulfilment through home and family. Signs of this shift in attititudes can be seen in the visual arts, with many more intimate domestic scenes being depicted on pottery and tombstones (Fig. 14, p. 37). During the war years, then, the sharp distinction between a masculine outdoor existence and the indoor world of women was beginning, very gradually, to be eroded.

This process was maintained in the century which followed the war. The political and economic decline experienced in Athens during those years meant that men's retreat from public life continued, and perceptions of the role of women were changing. But the ideal of seclusion, deeply rooted in the Athenian value-system, would have faded very slowly, and not without causing some tension between the sexes. The situation in post-war Britain during the 1950s and 60s was in some ways similar. Although economic and social changes meant that far more women were going out to work, it took a long time for this to be accepted as normal.

Did women go to the theatre?

In ancient Greece drama was largely a masculine affair: all the actors as well as the playwrights were male. But did women at least form part of the audience? Unfortunately we are unable to answer this question – the evidence is inconclusive. So we shall never know whether dramatists such as Euripides or Aristophanes had female responses partly in mind when they were inventing extraordinary characters such as Medea or Lysistrata.

Containers and other objects: women in vase-painting

In vase-paintings of the fifth century women are sometimes shown out of doors, drawing water from a fountain (Fig. 19), picking apples, or making offerings at a relative's tomb (Fig. 20, p. 76). Not surprisingly, however, most scenes show women inside the home: this was one of the ways in which the masculine ideal of female seclusion was promoted and reinforced. Within this domestic interior women are frequently surrounded

Fig. 20 A woman bringing offerings to a tomb. A jar of oil has been placed on the steps of the tomb; the basket held by the woman contains garlands and may also have been used to carry offerings of food. A white-ground *lekythos*, or oil-jar, c.440 BC.

by objects. These are of various types, but the most numerous and the most characteristic are the containers – the caskets and chests, jugs and jars, dishes and baskets which can be seen standing on the floor, hanging on the walls, or being handed to a woman by her maid (Fig. 9, p. 18).

These containers seem to have a number of meanings. As possessions, they represent the wealth of a household; when they are displayed in wedding processions (Fig. 12, p. 31), and perhaps on other occasions too, they symbolise the dowry, that substantial item of portable wealth which a bride brought with her when she was married. Containers could also be used for storing things and keeping them in order, so they also signify the married woman's function of organising the goods in a household, the task described so painstakingly by the model husband Ischomachos in Xenophon's treatise. Some receptacles refer, in addition, to specific domestic tasks. The most common item here is the *kalathos* or wool-basket (Fig. 18, p. 71), which brings to mind women's spinning and weaving activities even when there are no spindles, distaffs or looms in the picture.

Containers can also be seen as miniature interiors – they enclose things and hide them away. So Athenian viewers may have made a link between the objects which women in vase-paintings were holding and the wider domestic interior in which females themselves were contained. Perhaps at the same time they remembered that women too could be seen as containers. After all, a woman's womb was sometimes referred to as a 'vessel' or a 'wine-skin'; and the first female, Pandora, had been manufactured out of clay as though she were a jar. Like the vessels which surrounded them, women had the function of receiving, storing and protecting men's treasure, their embryonic sons. The *kalathos* too would almost certainly have been recognised as an emblem of the womb, for, as we have seen, a number of ideas connected the products of wool-working with the products of sexual intercourse; like other receptacles, the *kalathos* would have had both a direct meaning (women's manufacture of wool) and a symbolic one (their ability to give birth).

The more immediately enjoyable side of sexual activity is hinted at when a woman is handed a perfume-jar (Fig. 9, p. 18). As we learned from the encounter between Kinesias and Myrrhine in the *Lysistrata*, perfumed oil was used not just to make a woman more attractive, but also as a sex-aid; and one kind of perfume-bottle, an *alabastron*, was recognised as a phallic symbol. Many of the other objects associated with women, such as mirrors (Fig. 18) or jewel-cases and items of jewellery (Fig. 14, p. 37), refer in the same way to feminine adornment and sexual identity. Fruit and flowers (Fig. 18), evoking a woman's bloom or ripeness, have similar erotic connotations and remind us of the importance of her fertility. In later, more flamboyant paintings a strong atmosphere of eroticism is created by the lavish profusion of flowers, necklaces, perfume-jars, garlands and mirrors with which the women are encircled.

Often, a female figure is fixed to the domestic interior by a chair or a stool (Figs. 9 and 16, pp. 18, 42). The general rule when indoor scenes are depicted is that men are shown standing or, at a *symposium*, reclining, while women are sitting. In this way women's immobility and the restrictions that tied them to the home are underlined. The same message is relayed by the fact that most of the women are barefoot, since shoes seem to have been worn mainly out of doors. For this reason shoes were associated in particular with prostitutes, females who regularly left the home. Beds of course generally allude to a woman's sexual role: the emphasis placed on reproduction within the family means that they appear more frequently in the background of scenes featuring a bride than they do in brothel scenes.

Although pieces of furniture or household objects are generally all that is needed to denote an indoor setting, architectural elements such as doors and columns are sometimes included as well. These are used more often than not to signify a transition from exterior to interior space, or from one room of a house to another. In this way they mark the ultimate destination of the bride in a wedding procession (Fig. 12, p. 31), or the change in her social and sexual status implicit in her passage from living-room to bedroom.

Containers in the Parthenon frieze

Most of the women who lead the Panathenaic procession in the Parthenon frieze are carrying containers. In Fig. 5 (p. 9) the first woman is grasping an incense-burner, the next two have wine-jugs, and the last one holds a circular libation-dish, used for pouring drink-offerings to the gods. These objects would probably have called to mind a wide range of female functions, but in this particular context they referred above all to the women's religious role.

Women worshippers

Like unmarried women, wives had many important religious duties, and in this context their appearances outside the home would have been positively welcomed. Religion was the only area of activity where women in Athens were accorded a public role. As an expression of the community's strength and solidarity, these rites also represented the principal means by which females were integrated into the society whose continuance depended upon them.

Women's religious activities were carried out in a number of different settings. Within the *oikos* they took part in the daily honouring of the household's deities in prayer and sacrifice. They were also intimately involved in rituals which marked transitional stages in the human life-cycle, especially those relating to marriage, childbirth and death. Unsurprisingly, many of these rituals can be seen as an extension of the female's domestic role; the women of the household, for example, were responsible for washing, anointing and dressing corpses. As we have seen, women also played the most dramatic part in mourning a family's dead – a ritual which may well have fostered the female's reputation for emotional excess (Fig. 11, p. 26). Finally, offerings placed at regular intervals on a relative's tomb (Fig. 20, p. 76) were almost always brought by women. Indeed the cemetery, like the public fountain (Fig. 19, p. 74), was probably an important meeting-place for the community's womenfolk. To them this would certainly not have seemed too gruesome a location for the exchange of news, gossip, and stories.

Women were also members of religious associations devoted to the worship of particular divinities. In some of them, most famously those which practised the mysteries or secret rites of the god Dionysos, they were remarkably conspicuous. As a god of wine Dionysos was widely worshipped by Athenian men; but as a deity who was present in the kind of ecstasy induced by frenzied dancing and the rhythm of cymbals and drums, he was especially popular with women. These worshippers were known as Bacchae (Bacchic women) or maenads (mad women). It is very debatable to what extent Athenian females engaged in the sort of extravagant behaviour which Euripides attributes to the maenads of Thebes in his tragedy *Bacchae*; some of their more exotic activities, such as breast-feeding wolf-cubs or producing fountains of milk from the ground, are certainly imaginary. But the ecstatic worship of Dionysos may well have provided some women in Athens with an emotional outlet denied to them in their ordinary domestic lives. As Euripides' tragedy and many of the paintings of maenads illustrate, these rites would also have fuelled the masculine belief that women can all too readily pass over into a wild and uncontrolled state of being. In Fig. 8 (p.17) the maenad's loosened hair, her abandoned pose and her snakey head-dress and panther all suggest her closeness to the untamed world of nature.

Finally, and most significantly, women participated in the great public cults of Athens, celebrated in particular in elaborate civic festivals. Here they might take part on three different levels. They might be ordinary worshippers, joining in prayers and hymns, and producing a loud ritual cry when an animal was sacrificed. They might perform special religious tasks, such as helping to clean a cult-statue's ornaments. Lastly, they might be priestesses, the officials who were specially chosen to supervise the cult of a goddess and administer her sanctuary. In Athens there were more than forty of these, the most important being the priestess of

Athena (Fig. 6, p. 12), the only Athenian-born woman known on occasions to have exerted a political influence.

Most religious celebrations were open to both sexes, but there were some important festivals in Athens which were exclusive to women. The most notable of these was the Thesmophoria, an autumn festival of the goddess Demeter which lasted for three days. It was apparently restricted to the wives of citizens, and for the duration of the event they camped out in specially erected huts in the sanctuary. For many married women this would have been the only time in the year when they were able to spend a few nights away from home. One of its crucial rituals involved women who brought up the rotting remains of pigs and cakes from the underground chambers in which they had been buried some time previously. These were placed on altars, and farmers could take a portion and mix it with their seed-corn, which was planted shortly afterwards. Other rites of the festival included fasting, sitting on the ground, and a celebration held on the last day called 'Fair Birth'.

On one level the festival seems to have had the object of promoting fertility, both of crops and of women. While the use which it made of underground chambers calls to mind the links which we have already noted between the earth, containers and women's wombs, the Thesmophoria's broader significance lay in its acknowledgement of the vital contribution made by females to the well-being of the community. The whole event was organised by women referred to as 'magistrates', so for a few days Athenian wives were allowed a little freedom and even a little power. For once, they were in charge of their own affairs. This certainly did not amount to liberation, but it was enough to arouse familiar male anxieties. Myths in which men were castrated by female celebrants who caught them spying on the festival's rites found an echo in Aristophanes' comedy *Women celebrating the Thesmophoria*, in which the worshippers condemn the tragedian Euripides to death for slandering women in his plays. All kinds of women-only events, ranging from festivals to childbirth, seem to have had the effect of arousing men's suspicions and fears. This can probably be seen as a reflection of the tremendous importance which Athenian males unconsciously attributed to these female activities and functions.

Chapter 4

Goddesses and characters from myth

The Olympian Goddesses

Scores of deities, both male and female, were worshipped in Athens; but the divine scene was dominated by a ruling elite whose members were referred to as the twelve Olympians: there were six goddesses (Hera, Athena, Artemis, Aphrodite, Demeter, and Hestia) and six gods (Zeus, Poseidon, Apollo, Hermes, Ares, Hephaistos). All these deities were interrelated – the group included brothers and sisters, sons and daughters, aunts and uncles – so that they formed an extended family as well as a kind of governing council. The god Zeus was their acknowledged leader, although individual members of the team wielded tremendous power.

Five of these Olympian goddesses were depicted in the east section of the Parthenon frieze. They were shown sitting alongside the gods and waiting to greet the Panathenaic procession. Hestia, a stay-at-home goddess, does not appear: her place has been taken by Dionysos, a deity of particular importance to women. The east section of the frieze was originally positioned above the Parthenon's east porch, so that visitors to the building would have looked at it just before entering the temple and would have been reminded of the presence of the Olympians. Athena, the presiding deity of the Parthenon, is seated just to the right of the centre, with the blacksmith god Hephaistos to her right and the *peplos* to her left (Fig. 6, p. 12). Just to the left of the centre Athena's father Zeus sits on a throne next to his wife Hera (Fig. 15, p. 39). Sadly, the members of the Olympian group have been parted by circumstances. Most are now in the British Museum, but four of them (Poseidon, Apollo, Artemis, and a very badly damaged Aphrodite) are in the Acropolis Museum in Athens.

As both a family and a council the Olympian group provided a model for many of the institutions in Athenian society: on this basis they could be used for exploring tensions and conflicts which arose in real life. As personalities, too, the Olympians closely resembled human beings – their thoughts, emotions and reactions were in some ways very similar to those of real people. But there were also some crucial differences. As immortal, all-powerful beings the Olympians were blissfully free from many of the constraints and limitations which hampered the human race. This distinction is particularly significant in the case of the goddesses, who were seen as exercising considerable authority at a time when mortal women were politically and socially subordinate to men. Often in representations of goddesses the features which were being stressed were the ones which made them utterly unlike their female worshippers.

Yet these goddesses touched the lives of Athenian women in many important respects. Because of their links with ordinary females, most of them have already been encountered, in one guise or another, in Chapters 2 and 3. What follows is a summary of their main characteristics and functions.

Athena

The blend of masculine and feminine attributes displayed by the patron deity of Athens is probably her most striking feature. As the goddess who supervised the art of wool-working, Athena was intimately involved in the most characteristic of women's activities. This side of her operations was acknowledged in the manufacture of the Panathenaic *peplos* (Fig. 6, p. 12), just one of the numerous religious tasks performed in her honour by the young female residents of Athens. However, Athena is best known to most of us for her spirited participation in vigorous manly pursuits. She was a warrior, a military strategist, and a champion of heroes and defender of fortresses. She was also an outstanding technician, the inventor of the ship, the chariot, and the bridle. For this reason she was a close associate of Hephaistos, the metal-worker among the Olympians, who is seen sitting next to Athena on the Parthenon frieze (Fig. 6). As someone who excelled in *metis*, or 'cunning intelligence' (a better translation nowadays might be 'lateral thinking'), Athena was also a great friend of the wily hero Odysseus, to whom she lent her unstinting support in his attempts to return home after the Trojan War.

The goddess's gender-bending character was graphically demonstrated by her style of dress. She rarely went out without equipping herself with a helmet, breastplate and shield; but underneath all this masculine gear she always wore a woman's robe. This feminine element in her appearance was matched by her looks, which were never considered butch or ungainly. She was lovely and graceful, and the sight of her naked body sent the young man Teiresias into raptures, with disastrous consequences – as already mentioned – for his eyesight. For though she was physically alluring Athena was also a steadfast virgin who hotly resisted the sexual attentions, and even the admiring gazes, of the males with whom she associated.

The young women of Athens were clearly devoted to their goddess and made many offerings which recorded their gratitude for her protection. Her lifestyle, however, was in many ways quite different from theirs, for unlike them she was able to reject the roles of wife and mother. An awareness of the goddess's difference – her dynamism and her independence from male control – must have made her an object of admiration as well as affection among Athenian females. Athena was feminine and yet at the same time she was strong, untouched by the passivity and vulnerability so often associated with ordinary mortal women. Perhaps she helped to boost young women's confidence and increase their sense of self-worth.

Athena was also remote from ordinary feminine experience in another respect. She had no mother, for her father Zeus had swallowed his first wife Metis when she was pregnant, in response to a prophecy that any child born from this goddess would eventually usurp his position as ruler of gods and men. Through this act Zeus not only evaded the prophecy, but also absorbed the quality of *metis*, which he was to pass on to his daughter. Some time later he had a terrible headache, and when the blacksmith Hephaistos obligingly cracked open his skull with an axe a miniature Athena popped into view, already brandishing her weapons (Fig. 7, p. 15). This close association with her father was maintained throughout the goddess's subsequent career, and she often served as his ally in the power struggles which raged on Mount Olympus. So when Apollo at the trial of Orestes argued that the mother was not the true parent of the child, Athena was able to back him up: 'No mother gave me birth/I honour the male in all things, apart from marriage/With all my heart I am the child of the father.' (AESCHYLUS, *Eumenides* 736-8). At the end of the day the virgin goddess who had managed to escape a husband's domination was unswervingly loyal to a patriarchal system of government.

Many factors must have contributed to the Athenians' adoption of a stalwart virgin and motherless child as their patron divinity. Among them we can certainly count their impulse to dissociate the goddess who represented them from all the inherent weaknesses attributed to females. The deity who defended their fortress must not be subject to domination by any male other than the father. The goddess who nurtured the young heroes of Athens must not be tainted with the reputation for domestic violence which so frequently attached itself to biological mothers of both the divine and the human variety. Athena, the Warrior Maiden whose sterling qualities were so conspicuously celebrated in the Parthenon, was murderous only when she was confronted by enemies. Towards her friends she was unfailingly loyal and caring.

Artemis

An energetic hunting deity who haunted remote wooded hillsides, Artemis was the goddess who supervised the wilder side of femininity. At her sanctuary in Brauron she presided over the athletic exertions of young girls whose vigour would soon have to be tamed and harnessed if they were to meet the demands of marriage and motherhood. In myth, too, much of her time was spent with young women, since, unlike Athena, Artemis shunned the company of males and the bustling life of the city streets. But she resembled the divine patron of Athens in that she was a virgin, and had been allocated areas of responsibility which embraced both masculine and feminine concerns.

Like warfare, hunting was an activity which in real life was exclusive to men, and expertise in the pursuit and capture of one's prey was seen as a characteristically masculine accomplishment. As the virgin goddess of the hunt Artemis was able to promote the ideal of sexual self-control which sportsmen were bound to observe if they were to gain mastery over themselves and their environment. But as the divinity who superintended every aspect of childbearing Artemis was also intimately involved in the lives of young women – much more so than Athena. In this sphere of her operations the significance of the goddess's virginity is much less easy to understand. How could Artemis help women give birth when she herself had never experienced this event? Perhaps the answer lies in the passivity attributed to married women. As a hunter Artemis had to inflict wounds on animals, and as a goddess of childbirth she had to make women suffer. So, like Athena on the battlefield, she needed to be active rather than passive, she needed to cause pain rather than experience it. When mothers at Brauron dedicated their precious items of clothing to the goddess, they were probably thanking her for making their agonies bearable. She had wounded them, but she had allowed them to survive.

Hera

As the consort of Zeus and the goddess of marriage Hera had a vital role in most Greek communities. In Athens special sacrifices were made to her in the month *Gamelion* (our January, roughly), the 'wedding month' when many unions were celebrated. The goddess was highly revered, yet most Athenian women would have been well aware that in myth Hera's own marriage was pictured as a stormy affair. In Homer's *Iliad* she appears as a typical nagging wife, who keeps a jealous watch over all her husband's activities, and is especially outraged by his numerous extra-marital affairs. The many illegitimate offspring fathered by Zeus are often the victims of terrible acts of vengeance engineered by Hera. The hero Heracles, for example, has to endure the burden of twelve appalling labours imposed on him as a result of Hera's machinations. Far from being a loving mother – she has a particularly tetchy relationship with her son Hephaistos – the goddess is frequently awarded in myth the role of the wicked stepmother.

Marriage, as we have learned, would rarely have been viewed by Athenian women as an unalloyed blessing, and they may not have been unduly disturbed by the problematical character of the goddess who supervised it. But marriage was also central to women's experience, and in worshipping Hera they would have been honouring a deity who represented, for good or ill, a major element in their lives. Indeed, the prominence given to Hera's veil-lifting gesture in the Parthenon frieze (Fig. 15, p. 39) demonstrates that marriage was recognised as a crucial institution not only by women but by Athenian society as a whole.

Aphrodite

Aphrodite was the goddess of sexual love, and as such she had links with most of the females living in Athens. She was a particular favourite with the city's many prostitutes but also supervised the sexual life of married women, and in vase-paintings she was pictured with growing frequency helping to adorn young brides. This aspect of her activities must have been viewed with a degree of uneasiness by some Athenian men. Aphrodite herself was married to the blacksmith god Hephaistos, but was far from being a faithful wife, having had well-publicised affairs with a number of lovers, both divine and mortal, including a gorgeous youth named Adonis. She also promoted adulterous relationships between human beings, and had famously arranged for the Trojan prince Paris to elope with the beautiful Helen. So the role model presented to her female worshippers was clearly somewhat dubious.

Like some of the other Olympian goddesses, Aphrodite adopted standards of behaviour which were totally different from the ones imposed on ordinary Athenian females. The young women who performed secret rites for the goddess prior to their marriages must have realised that they were being initiated into the sexual side of their relationships by a deity whose lifestyle they could not hope to imitate; but once they were married their worship of Aphrodite would provide them with an outlet for pent-up emotions and desires. At the annual festival of the Adonia women mourned the death of the goddess's young lover Adonis with extravagant displays of grief. Athenian men were horrified when the wails and shouts of these female worshippers could be heard above the voices of speakers in the Assembly during a debate on a crucial military campaign (ARISTOPHANES, Lysistrata 389 ff).

In the course of the fourth century a more relaxed attitude towards Aphrodite began to emerge. The increasingly sensual treatment of the goddess's figure in sculpture (Fig. 10, p. 22) was matched by a more explicit appreciation of the emotional and erotic aspects of married life. Men were assigning greater value to their personal experiences, and although wives were certainly not allowed the same sexual freedoms as Aphrodite, the contribution made by the goddess of love to marital relationships was freely acknowledged and celebrated.

Demeter

Demeter, the goddess of corn and cultivation (Fig. 13, p. 36), was featured most prominently in myth as the mother who mourned the loss of her daughter Persephone. Of the six Olympian goddesses she was the only one who provided her female worshippers with a positive image of motherhood. No doubt many women would have found the story of her vigorous defence of her offspring inspiring, although none could have hoped to imitate her achievements and negotiate the return of her daughter after marriage.

In Athens Demeter was honoured in a number of important rites, most notably the Eleusinian Mysteries and the women-only festival of the Thesmophoria. The latter event in particular would have brought women exceptionally close to the goddess. At the same time the link which the celebrations made between women's childbearing function and the masculine activity of agriculture would have made them aware of the responsibility which they shared with their menfolk for securing the well-being of Athens.

Hestia

The third Olympian virgin, Hestia, was worshipped throughout Greece as the goddess of the hearth. Like Athena and Artemis she had vowed never to marry, and had received in compensation a central place in every Greek household. The hearth – which was called a *hestia*, and was located in the middle of a room – was a kind of family altar and was the focal point for many domestic rituals. As we have seen, a bride was conducted to the *hestia* when she first arrived in her new home, and babies were carried around it when they were a few days old. It symbolised the stable core of the *oikos*, and it is not at all surprising that it should have been represented by a female divinity noted for her immobility.

While other deities were out and about, Hestia remained at home on Mount Olympus keeping the fire alight. As a result she had very few adventures, and played only a small role in myth. Of the three virgin goddesses, she was the one who came closest to providing a role model for young unmarried women who were sheltered from the outside world. Yet Hestia was widely honoured, not just in Athenian homes, but also at the communal hearth in the *prytaneion*, a kind of town hall near the civic centre where a fire was kept perpetually burning. The permanence and security which the goddess guaranteed reached out from the *oikos* into the very heart of the *polis*, and in this way the significance of women's domestic role was publicly acknowledged.

Mythological females in the Parthenon sculptures

In the metopes, the rectangular slabs above the outer columns of the Parthenon, four mythological battles were represented. All of them in one way or another symbolised the struggle between civilisation and barbarism. In one of them, the conflict between the Gods and the Giants, the combatants were all divine. In the other three the defenders of civilisation were heroes, mortal men of exceptional prowess and courage who had earned the right to be worshipped after their deaths. Naturally, the heroes had the starring roles in these battle-scenes; but in all three of them women too were given a significant role.

'Amazons who live without men' (AESCHYLUS, *Suppliant women 287*)

The sculptures in the west pediment of the Parthenon (Fig. 3, p. 8) showed Athena's victory over the god of the sea, Poseidon, in a contest held to decide which of them should become patron deity of Athens. In the metopes below the pediment a battle between the Greeks and the mythical warrior women known as the Amazons was represented. This combination of episodes would have reminded the viewer of the differences between gods and mortals. In the divine sphere a female champion like Athena could gain supremacy over a male opponent; but in the world of humans women could not hope to emulate the goddess's achievements. Every Greek viewer would have known that when the Amazons encountered the Greeks on the battlefield they were always defeated.

The Amazons were reputed to have lived in Themiskyra, a city on the south-eastern shore of the Black Sea. This meant that they were non-Greeks, a point of considerable importance, because like foreigners in many modern-day myths they did everything the wrong way round. *Barbaroi*, or foreigners, were seen as fundamentally different from the Greeks and, in most people's view, vastly inferior to them. Women too, when compared with men, were thought of as different and inferior, and so they could easily be identified with the barbarians. As foreign females, then, the Amazons were doubly damned. Their way of life was the complete opposite of the one led by civilised Greeks.

In Amazonland women took on the masculine role of warfare, and wore masculine attire such as helmets, greaves, and breastplates. They were also in charge of the government of their state, for they lived entirely without men. When the annual love-ins which they conducted with men from the neighbouring Gargarian tribe resulted in the birth of girl babies, these were reared by their mothers; boys were handed over to the Gargarians. So the Amazons departed radically from Greek social values, both in being sexually promiscuous and refusing to marry, and in regarding female offspring more highly than males. According to a number of Roman writers the Amazons used to cut off the right breasts of their daughters to prevent them from getting in their way when they were fighting. This may have been invented in order to account for the women's name, since 'A-mazon' could be translated as 'without-a-breast'; but no author of the classical period mentions this aspect of their appearance, and in vase-paintings and sculptures Amazons are always shown with the normal two breasts.

There is no evidence that the Amazons, as described in classical literature, ever existed. No Greek writer claims ever to have met an Amazon. In fact, most people who record their activities believe that they lived long ago, in the time of the Trojan War; since then their race has died out, which is taken as proof that women cannot survive indefinitely without men. 'Who could ever believe that an army of women, or a city, or a tribe could ever be organised without men...?' asks the geographer Strabo (11.5.3). Comments like this give us one clue as to why the myth may have been invented in the first place. It offers a demonstration of why women need men, when on the face of it, provided they have sex occasionally, they can manage perfectly well without them.

Nowadays when we refer to women as Amazons we tend to be focussing on the sporty or combative qualities of their mythical fore-runners; an 'Amazonian' woman is one who is strong, vigorous and well developed, like the female Gladiators on television. The Greeks, too, obviously thought that women in combat gear were sexy. The Amazon scenes on the Parthenon, though still in position on the building, are so badly damaged that all the detail has been lost. But in similar scenes from a temple of Apollo at Bassai (Fig. 21, p. 90), now in the British Museum, the Amazons are shown in a series of contorted poses which draw our attention to their voluptuous bottoms and breasts, often left exposed by flying drapery.

Much as the Greeks must have enjoyed these displays of muscular femininity, for them the story would have carried more negative connotations. As separatists who tried to live without men the Amazons provided a warning about the female sex's potential for subverting the norms of civilised society. In this respect their closest counterpart in our own society is not the female athlete or fighter but the single mother, who is also seen by some people as presenting a threat to our traditional way of life. But the Amazons were fictional, and the Greeks could supply the story with what seemed to them an appropriate ending – so the myth offered them the reassurance that any group of women that attempted to 'go it alone' in this way was doomed to failure.

For although the female warriors were immensely successful and conquered large tracts of territory, they were never able to get the better of the Greeks. The mythical heroes Heracles and Theseus both conducted successful expeditions against them. The latter's capture of an Amazon queen provoked a wholesale Amazonian invasion of Athens, which was halted by Theseus after the women had launched an assault on the Acropolis. In the fifth century this event was seen as a mythical precedent for the two Persian invasions of Greece in 490 and 480 BC; the parallel between the Amazons and the real-life barbarians was stressed when vase-painters dressed the women up in oriental clothes and supplied them with Persian weaponry such as bows and arrows. Another myth relates how an Amazon queen called Penthesileia brought an army to Troy to help defend the city against the Greeks. On the battlefield she was confronted by the hero Achilles, who impaled her on his spear, and then fell in love with her as she lay dying.

In all these episodes the Amazons are overpowered by a combination of military and sexual strength. In another story, recounted by the historian Herodotus (4.110-118), the women are disarmed by their own erotic desires. When a contingent of Amazons arrived in the territory of the Scythians, to the north of the Black Sea, and started pillaging their settlements, the local youths decided to fend them off by conducting a campaign of seduction. They established a camp close to the one set up by the Amazons:

Fig. 21 Amazons fighting Greeks, from the frieze of the temple of Apollo at Bassai, c 420 BC.

A Scythian young man ran into one of the Amazons when she wandered out of the camp by herself, and seized her in his arms. She did not push him away, but allowed him to have his way with her. Since they could not understand each other's language, she made signs with her hands to indicate that he should come back to the same spot the next day bringing another young man (making a sign for two), and she would bring another woman.

(HERODOTUS 4.113)

This blind date process spread, and became so popular that after a while the two camps were combined into one. Eventually the Amazons and the Scythians settled down together and, according to Herodotus, became the ancestors of the Sauromatian race, who lived in the steppes of Central Asia. In the historian's own day, he tells us, Sauromatian females still went hunting on horseback, engaged in warfare, and wore masculine clothes. They even had a law which forbade a woman to marry until she had killed an enemy in battle.

This last part of Herodotus' account seems to be confirmed by archaeological excavations, which have uncovered Sauromatian female graves of the sixth to fourth centuries BC containing weapons and armour. One of these burials was unearthed at the beginning of 1997, and was greeted in British newspapers with headlines such as 'Greeks may have been right about the Amazons'. In ancient Greece travellers' tales about the strange customs of real-life Sauromatian women may well have helped to create the myth of the Amazons. But the newspaper headline is misleading – in Herodotus' story the Amazons are certainly not said to be identical with the female Sauromatians. Only when the fictional warrior women had given up their separatist ways and been brought back into the fold of the nuclear family could they be considered to belong to a viable race of people. This for him was surely the value of the tale which he tells – it shows that for one reason or another women cannot live without men.

Lapiths versus Centaurs

In the west metopes of the Parthenon the barbarian enemy was repre-sented by women. In the metopes on the south side of the building the barbarians were monsters, the part-horse part-human creatures known as the Centaurs. Perithoos, the king of the Lapith tribe, was foolish enough to invite a group of Centaurs, who were notoriously drunken and randy, to his wedding feast. His guests behaved according to form, drank too much wine and tried to rape the bride and all the other females present (Fig. 22). The Lapiths resisted them strenuously and managed to rescue their womenfolk; and in this way they demonstrated the importance of marriage as a civilising institution. A wedding had been disrupted by the

Fig. 22 A Centaur carries off a Lapith woman. A metope from the south side of the Parthenon, c.440 BC.

bestial and promiscuous sexuality of the Centaurs, but order had been restored, and the women had been able to resume their rightful place as the beneficiaries of male guardianship within marriage. So the Lapith women were quite unlike the Amazons represented in the earlier set of metopes: they were helpless and passive, but they were also chaste, and instead of being opposed by men they received their care and protection.

Helen and the sack of Troy

In the prelude to the story told in the north metopes a marriage had been disrupted by a foreigner, the Trojan prince Paris. When acting as a judge in a divine beauty contest he had accepted a bribe from Aphrodite, and after choosing her as the winner had been rewarded with the love of another man's wife, the wondrously beautiful Helen. This was the incident which sparked off the Trojan War. The metopes depicted the events which took place ten years later, when the city of Troy was sacked by the Greeks. In one of the scenes, badly damaged but still just about visible on the temple, we witness the moment when the marriage of Helen and the Greek hero Menelaus was reinstated. The angry husband rushes towards Helen brandishing his sword, and she takes refuge at a statue of a deity. But between them stands Aphrodite, interceding with Menelaus on her protégée's behalf. Every Greek knew from Homer's *Odyssey* what the outcome of this encounter would be – love was triumphant, and Helen returned to Greece to resume her position as Menelaus' wife.

In Homer's poems Helen is an ambiguous personality, presented sometimes as the instigator of the Trojan War, at others as the helpless victim of Aphrodite. By the fifth century, however, attitudes towards adulterous wives were hardening, and in Athens at least Helen took on a much more menacing aspect. These are the words used to describe her in one of the tragedies of the period:

> Swerving from her course,
> she steered her marriage towards a bitter end,
> blasting the children of Priam with ruin and evil
> when Zeus god of guests brought her among them,
> a bride drenched in tears, a Fury, a fiend.
> (AESCHYLUS, *Agamemnon* 744-9)

In these verses it is the terrible violence caused by Helen's betrayal which is the focus of attention. In the north metopes of the Parthenon the final throes of this violence were represented; but at the same time the viewer was invited to anticipate the restoration of order which would accompany Menelaus' recovery of his wife. The civilised marriage practices of the Greeks had been thrown into disarray by a foreigner's treacherous theft of a bride, but now at last this wrong had been righted.

Chapter 5
Other women

Metics, or resident aliens

The women represented in the Parthenon frieze who walked at the head of the Panathenaic procession were the daughters and wives of Athenian citizens. By no means all of the women in this sector of society came from affluent families, but in one degree or another they were separated from the other females living in the city by important social barriers.

Metics were non-Athenians – mostly Greeks from other states – who had been given special permission to reside in Athens. The majority of metic men worked in manufacturing or retail industries or as tenant farmers, but a few managed to make large fortunes as industrialists or bankers. All of them were excluded from citizenship and the right to own land. Most of the women in the metic class would have been the spouses or children of these men, and they too suffered from a significant social disability. After 451, when Pericles introduced his new law stipulating that a man needed both an Athenian mother and an Athenian father in order to qualify for citizenship, a metic woman's chances of finding a husband from the citizen class would have been very much reduced.

Many metic females would have had jobs outside the home, and some may have worked alongside citizen women as casual farm labourers, market stallholders, and so on. In situations like this the women would probably not have been aware of any tremendous distinction between them – their everyday lives would have been very similar, and they would have mixed together quite freely; but the exclusion of metic women from religious events such as the Thesmophoria festival may well have produced a sense of social inferiority. On the other hand metic females may have enjoyed more freedom of movement than many citizen women. Although resident aliens probably adopted rules of behaviour similar to those followed by the Athenians, the fact that their womenfolk could not give birth to citizens may have meant that the protection of their chastity was not quite such a major issue.

A small minority of metic women had come to Athens independently and registered in their own right as resident aliens. Most of them worked as prostitutes, a profession which will be discussed in a later section.

Slaves

By the mid-fifth century about one third or more of the total population of Athens consisted of slaves. The majority were males who worked on their owners' farms or in manufacturing workshops. But most 'middle-income' citizens would probably have been able to afford the additional expense of a slave-girl, like the one kept by Euphiletos, to help their wives with domestic chores. More affluent households would certainly have owned a number of domestic servants, although we never hear of any home which has more than a total of ten. In these families female slaves could have aspired to more specialised roles, such as housekeeper, cook or nurse (Fig. 16, p. 42). In the well-ordered household of the wealthy Ischomachos there was a housekeeper who helped to manage the junior slaves and organise the storage and distribution of goods. When they were appointing her, he and his wife were careful to choose someone who was restrained in her eating, drinking and sleeping habits, and in her behaviour towards the opposite sex. 'We also taught her to be loyal to us by making her a partner in all our joys, and by inviting her to share our troubles' (XENOPHON, *Household management* 9.12).

Sometimes female slaves would have become their mistresses' confidantes or the much-loved companions of the children they had nursed. Just occasionally they may have been called upon to perform more dangerous duties, and act as go-betweens in extra-marital affairs. But this would have been a risky enterprise, as we learn from the crisis in Euphiletos' home, where the maid eventually informed on the lovers when she was threatened with a whipping.

Brutal punishments of this kind may have been fairly common and the position of a slave would seldom have been an enviable one. In law they were treated as mere possessions, and a man could bequeath a slave to someone else in his will, as Aristotle did. But in situations where both a mistress and a slave-girl were more or less confined to the home the women would often have relied on each other for companionship and even for affection. The sadness of the slave-girls who are frequently depicted on their mistresses' tombstones (Fig. 14, p. 37) would not always have been a hollow artistic convention.

Prostitutes

As a trading centre with a busy port, Athens possessed a plentiful supply of prostitutes. Most of these were female, although male brothels were apparently quite common. Sexual partners of a wide variety of types were available. The most affordable were the *pornai*, the prostitutes working in the low-grade brothels, who were generally slaves owned by the brothel-keeper. Sometimes they used to sit outside in the street, topless if the weather was warm, enticing passers-by to enter their establishments. Female dancers, flute-players and acrobats, hired to provide entertainment at *symposia*, often performed sexual services as well. Most of these were probably slaves, but as skilled artists they would have been more expensive. At the top end of the market were the women known as *hetairai*, or 'female companions'. These were sophisticated beauties, occasionally Athenians but more often metics, who charged very high prices for an evening spent in their company. They formed the only significant group of economically independent women in Athens.

Most men in the city could probably have afforded to visit a prostitute from time to time, and the practice may not have been regarded as anything out of the ordinary. According to one law-court speaker, the sons of some of the most respectable men in the city used to give themselves nicknames referring to the size of their equipment, and had passionate love affairs with *hetairai.* Sometimes they got into fights over their mistresses. 'That's just the way young men behave', was a typical verdict (DEMOSTHENES 54.14).

But it might be going too far to assume that most men made regular use of the sexual services which were obtainable outside the home: even the liveliest of drinking sessions did not, it seems, automatically end in sex. At the conclusion of an upper-class party described in Xenophon's *Symposium* the guests watched an erotic ballet which featured the arrival of Dionysos in the bedroom of his bride Ariadne. The spectators were very enthusiatic about this performance. When it was over the ones who were married hurried home to their wives, while those who were single resolved to marry as quickly as possible. Socrates and his friends went for a walk.

A prostitute goes into retirement

Sometimes when people retired they dedicated the tools of their trade to an appropriate deity. This is a poem which commemorated a dedication by a prostitute:

> Now past fifty, and sated at last,
> Nikias that lover of love
> has hung up in Aphrodite's temple

her sandals, her mane of loosened hair,
her shining mirror that always told the truth,
her costly girdle, and the things men never mention.
Here you can see a complete exhibition of Love.

(PHILETAS, *The Greek anthology* 6.210)

Theodote

Socrates once went to visit a *hetaira* named Theodote who was renowned
for her beauty. When he arrived he found her posing for a portrait painter,
wearing a splendid gown and plenty of jewellery. Her mother was sitting
beside her, and she too was very well dressed. The house was lavishly
furnished and had a number of charming slave-girls.

Did Theodote derive her income from a farming estate?, the philosopher
asked, with his tongue in his cheek. Or from renting out a house? Or from
a manufacturing workshop? No, said Theodote.

'When someone becomes my friend and wants to help me,
he provides me with a livelihood.'

(XENOPHON, *Memorabilia* 3.11.4)

Neaira

Very few prostitutes would have been as fortunate as Theodote. One of
the most depressing stories which we hear is that of an ex-slave called
Neaira who while living in Corinth had been purchased from a brothel-
keeper by two young customers. When they were about to be married
they offered to let her buy her freedom, generously allowing her a dis-
count on her original purchase price. In order to raise the money Neaira
organised a whip-round among her old clients, and then came to Athens
with the one who had contributed the most, a man named Phrynion.

Phrynion introduced his mistress to fashionable society in the city,
and used to take her along to *symposia*. Her behaviour on these occasions
caused a great deal of scandal. According to her accusers Phrynion used
to have sex with Neaira in front of the other guests, and at one particularly
wild party she consorted with a large number of the men present, including some of the slaves. Eventually she left Phrynion, and set up house
with an Athenian called Stephanos.

Later, in about 340 BC, Neaira was brought to court on a charge of living with Stephanos as his wife, for by that time it was illegal for citizens to
marry non-Athenians. Her accusers were particularly shocked by the fact

that Stephanos had passed off Neaira's children as his own, and had twice given her daughter in marriage to Athenian citizens. In an emotional appeal they urged the members of the jury to remember that their own wives, daughters, and mothers 'should not be held in the same esteem as a prostitute...or appear to be sharing their privileges with a woman who in so many obscene ways has consorted so many times a day with so many men...' (DEMOSTHENES 59.114). Needless to say, no-one took any account of the fact that as a slave Neaira had had no choice at all about becoming a prostitute in the first place.

Aspasia

It is no coincidence that the most famous woman in fifth-century Athens was someone who was widely reputed to have earned her living as a *hetaira* and a brothel-keeper. Aspasia was born in the eastern Greek city of Miletus and emigrated to Athens at a fairly young age. We cannot be certain that she had ever in reality worked in the sex industry, but once she had become the mistress of the statesman Pericles she became an easy target for the smutty jokes made by comic playwrights. After divorcing his wife Pericles lived with Aspasia for about fifteen years, up to his death in 429 BC. According to one later writer:

> His affection for Aspasia was clearly of a sexual nature. His own wife was a close relative.... Later their married life became disagreeable, and with his wife's consent Pericles arranged for her to marry another man. He took Aspasia into his home and loved her dearly. Every day on leaving for public business and on returning home in the evening he used to kiss her.
>
> (PLUTARCH, *Life of Pericles* 24)

Aspasia was also renowned for her intelligence and her political acumen. We are told that the philosopher Socrates used to take his students to visit her, and that 'his friends brought their wives along to listen to her talk, even though she managed a business that was far from dignified or even respectable, since she ran a training school for young prostitutes' (PLUTARCH, *Life of Pericles* 24). In one of Plato's dialogues Socrates, in what is admittedly a joking frame of mind, claims that Aspasia used to conduct seminars on public speaking, and even credits her with having been the true author of Pericles' famous funeral speech (PLATO, *Menexenus* 235e-236b).

No well-bred Athenian woman would have behaved in this way, of course. But Aspasia was not an Athenian, and she was free from many of the restrictions which hampered the lives of local women. As someone who could be safely consigned to the category of outsider, she did not pose a serious threat to the Athenian value-system. So she could be allowed to win fame for herself as an active participant in both verbal and sexual exchanges with men. Although very few Athenian citizens would have wanted their own womenfolk to follow Aspasia's example, some of them nevertheless admired her. Others clearly saw her behaviour as shocking.

Like some of the present-day wives of prime ministers or presidents, Aspasia was widely regarded as having influenced Pericles' domestic and foreign policies. We have no way of knowing whether this was true or not; but gossip of this kind would certainly have provided Pericles' political opponents with plenty of useful ammunition. The vicious caricatures of his mistress which appeared in the comedies of the period combined jokes about her career in prostitution with references to her interference in politics. On one occasion, we are told, Aspasia was prosecuted for impiety and procuring. At her trial she was passionately defended by Pericles himself, and the prosecution failed.

Chapter 6
Conclusion

In our investigation of the women of Classical Athens we have encountered a number of personalities who failed to conform to the ideal of the modest and submissive female. On the divine level of operations Athena was by no means the only goddess whose pattern of behaviour placed her in a different category from ordinary mortal women. Down among the humans the Amazons went even further, and adopted a lifestyle which was the complete opposite of the one laid down for respectable Athenian wives. In tragedy and comedy female characters regularly engaged in activities which would have horrified most of the men in the audience; and in some quarters similar outrage was stirred up by real-life women such as Aspasia.

Most of these female personalities had been invented by men. Even Aspasia could be said to some extent to be a male creation. Her status as a non-Athenian and a mistress placed her beyond the moral boundaries established for citizen women, and helped to earn her a reputation for sexual promiscuity. Through characters such as these the Athenians were constructing negative guidelines for female behaviour – Athenian women could not hope to become goddesses, and as far as possible were to be prevented from turning themselves into Amazons, Medeas, or Aspasias.

Today it is difficult for us fully to understand the reasons why Athenian men were so concerned about women. The factors involved would have been very complex, but among them we can include the enormous power which the democratic system had vested in male citizens, and the gulf which this created between the dominant group and the rest of the population. Many elements in their society and culture encouraged Athenian men to view themselves as civilised, active and self-controlled. This definition was underpinned by images of 'the other' – of beings on the opposite side of the gulf who represented everything which they themselves were not. Foremost among these were women, regarded as potentially wild and unrestrained creatures who were badly in need of masculine guidance and control. Once they had been anchored within the boundaries of the civilised *polis* their energies could be harnessed, and they could perform the child-bearing and religious functions on which the security and stability of the community depended.

Men in Athens were well aware that these boundaries could easily be overstepped. Very few Athenian females were as violent as Medea or as sexually promiscuous as Aspasia was rumoured to be. But when a woman popped out of the house to visit a neighbour, or earned some extra money by helping with the harvest, or occasionally let herself go in her dancing for Dionysos, she was confirming male suspicions about her capacity for disruption. The woman herself, however, may have seen this as a small price to pay for a few hours of freedom. Mild acts of rule-bending like these would have created a space in her life for female companionship, and given her a sense of psychological independence from the men in her family.

During the Peloponnesian War opportunities for manipulating the code of female behaviour became more plentiful. The social and cultural gap between male citizens and their womenfolk was very slowly beginning to narrow. In the course of the following century political and economic decline brought hardship to some, and disillusionment to many. But for the women of Athens it also meant a tentative easing of some of the constraints imposed on them during the years when their *polis* was at the height of its wealth and power.

Suggestions for Further Study

1. Why do you think that the chastity of women was so important to the Athenians? Was this the only reason why they developed an ideal of seclusion for women? What were the elements in their culture which stressed that 'women's place was in the home'? In what ways did women manage to evade the pressure to remain indoors?

2. Would the life of a *hetaira* really have been preferable to that of a respectable Athenian woman? What advantages did the Athenian woman enjoy compared with the other members of the female population?

3. Why do you think that Athenian women were given such an important role in religious worship? Does this contradict the notion of seclusion?

4. Make a list of the female mythological figures which you have come across, including the goddesses. In what ways did they depart from the standards set for ordinary mortal women? Why do you think this was the case? What aspects of their activities and behaviour would have been meaningful for ordinary women?

5. Which of our sources suggest that women were not always submissive? Do you think that some women had power in the home?

6. What were the various rituals involved in marriage, and how did they relate to the other aspects of a woman's life?

7. Can we believe what Aristophanes tells us about women?

8. Do you think that the treatment of women in Athens reflects badly on Athenian culture?

9. Does our practice of studying women as a separate category tend to confirm the notion that women are a 'special case' and ought to be treated differently from men? Do we really need 'Women in...' books?

Suggestions for Further Reading

L. Archer, S. Fischer, and M. Wyke, eds., *Women in Ancient Societies: an Illusion of the Night* (Macmillan, 1994).
This collection of essays includes chapters on women philosophers, women and medicine, and the Greek theory of gender.

S. Blundell, *Women in Ancient Greece* (British Museum Press, 1995).
A general book dealing with the lives of Greek women, and their portrayal in poetry, drama, and the visual arts, during the archaic and classical periods. Although much of the evidence is drawn from Athens, the poems of Homer and Hesiod and the women of Sparta are also discussed.

A. Cameron and A. Kuhrt, eds., *Images of Women in Antiquity* (Routledge, 1983, 1993).
Another collection of essays, which among other topics deals with women in vase-painting, Greek housing, and women's relationship with the goddess Artemis.

G. Clark, *Women in the Ancient World. Greece and Rome. New Surveys in the Classics, no.21* (Oxford University Press, 1987).
A short but lively book which gives an overview of the biological, domestic and social roles of Greek and Roman women.

E. Fantham, H.P. Foley, N.B. Kampen, S.B. Pomeroy, H.A. Shapiro, *Women in the Classical World: Image and Text* (Oxford University Press, 1994).
A collection of essays on Greek and Roman women. There are chapters on women in Athens and Sparta, on medicine, and on the Amazons.

R. Garland, *The Greek Way of Life: from Conception to Old Age* (Duckworth, 1990).
A book dealing with everyday life which includes detailed discussions of conception, pregnancy and childbirth.

R. Hawley and B. Levick, eds., *Women in Antiquity. New Assessments.* (Routledge, 1995).

The topics covered in this collection of essays include family life in the classical *polis*, Pandora, women's religious rituals, and the cult of Demeter and Persephone.

R. Just, *Women in Athenian Law and Life.* (Routledge, 1989).

A detailed treatment of the rules and regulations relating to marriage, property and inheritance, seclusion, and personal relationships.

M.R. Lefkowitz and M.B. Fant, eds., *Women's Life in Greece and Rome* (Johns Hopkins University Press, 1992).

A very useful source book. A wide-ranging selection of extracts from Greek and Roman texts, translated into English.

S.B. Pomeroy, *Goddesses, Whores, Wives and Slaves.* (Robert Hale, 1975).

The first work on women in Greece and Rome published after the advent of the post-war women's movement. The chapters relating to Greek women deal with goddesses and gods, the archaic period, Classical Athens, images of women in literature, and the Hellenistic period.

E.D. Reeder, ed., *Pandora. Women in Classical Greece.* (The Walters Art Gallery, Baltimore and Princeton University Press, 1995).

An exhibition catalogue with superb illustrations, it has excellent essays on Pandora, sorceresses, wedding images, and the public and private lives of women; it discusses many aspects of the treatment of women in vase-paintings, including women as animals, scenes showing the pursuit of women, women and containers, Amazons and maenads, and women and textiles.

P. Schmitt Pantel, ed., *From Ancient Goddesses to Christian Saints,* Vol.1 of *A History of Women in the West*, edited by G.Duby and M.Perrot (Harvard University Press, 1992).

This collection of essays includes useful chapters on women in vase-painting and on women's religious rituals.

F.I. Zeitlin, *Playing the Other. Gender and Society in Classical Greek Literature* (University of Chicago Press, 1996).

Essays on the representation of the feminine in poetry and in particular in Athenian drama.

Index of main topics